mediterranean

contents

introduction

Why eat a Mediterranean diet? Because it's packed full of delicious and healthy ingredients. Tuck into a daily dose of fresh fish, nuts, fresh vegetables, olive oil and fruit, and studies have shown you may even live longer, so there's that to consider too. But for most of us, Mediterranean food is loved for the dishes and flavours that have become part of daily life wherever in the world we live. With over 200 recipes in this book, you can learn how to make these meals at home for all the family to enjoy.

In the Greek section, recreate easy-as-you-like versions of classic Greek dishes such as moussaka, spanakopita, slow-cooked lamb and dolmades, and dish out the best Greek salad, tzatziki and fresh fish and calamari for dinner. Enjoy this food on hot summer days and nights, with the barbecue sizzling.

Pizza, pasta, lasagne, gelati. It's hard not to love Italian food, but you don't need to eat at a restaurant to enjoy it. In the Italian section, you'll find simple recipes for familiar Italian-style stews and grilled meats, as well as pizza, pasta and gnocchi variations to suit all tastes.

Lebanese food is famous for the mighty falafel, and in this book you'll find a few variations of that national dish that you can easily recreate at home. Add tabouleh on the side, or a chickpea salad, and finish off with a rose water pudding, and you'll be forgiven for thinking you are miles away from home.

You might think Turkish food is all about the meat - kebabs, more kebabs, meatballs, or flatbreads topped with mince. But beans and eggplant play a key role in Turkish food too, and have the making of great side salads to accompany the meaty mains that are also ideal for cooking on the barbie.

Spanish food is known for its sharability – small plates of tapas and large jugs of sangria all round. It's surprisingly easy to create your own Spanish-style tapas at home, with easy recipes in this book for garlicky prawns, breaded mushrooms and crispy croquettes. Or learn how to make a classic no-fuss Spanish omelette or paella.

The food of Morocco may be summed up in one dish: tagine. But there are so many varieties, and you'll find beef, lamb, chicken, fish and veggie versions in this chapter. Ideal for snuggling up on a winter's night. Just add couscous.

All this – in 6 key ingredients or less.

how to use this book

6 Key Ingredients

The recipes in this book have been created to make life easier for you in the kitchen. That's why we decided to make them using just 6 key ingredients, or less. This should help ensure that your road to efficient, simple meal preparation is stress free with delicious results that all the family can enjoy.

We define a key ingredient as something you might not always have in your fridge or pantry, and you may therefore need to buy beforehand.

These key ingredients are illustrated on each recipe page, so you can see at a glance which recipes include ingredients that you love or fancy eating for dinner tonight.

Staples

Most recipes also require some fridge and/or pantry staple items. While everybody is different and one person's staple is another person's shopping list, we have devised a list of items that we feel it's reasonable, and sensible, to stock up on for everyday cooking. This list covers basic condiments (salt, pepper, oil and vinegar) as well as baking essentials (flour, sugar, etc). We've chosen essential items that are regularly stocked in a family kitchen. See the next page for a full illustration of the pantry and fridge staples you will need.

The ingredients list for each recipe indicates first the key ingredients, then, if applicable, any staples required and optional ingredients you can choose to include. Optional ingredients are often garnishes, which are nice to have but not essential to the dish. Or 'love it-hate it' ingredients, such as coriander or red onion, if the dish can be made without them.

A note about eggs – eggs are included as a staple item when only 1 or 2 eggs are required and they do not comprise the main element of the dish. In the case of a frittata or quiche, for example, eggs are the main ingredient and have been included as a key ingredient.

We've devised some handy icons to accompany the recipes in this book and provide you with useful information on how to prepare the meals, such as cooking times, dietary exclusions and serve sizes. The following key explains the simple icons that you will find in the book.

 The number icon indicates the number of people we estimate the recipe to serve.

 The clock icon indicates how long a recipe takes to prepare and cook, so that's the total time we estimate it will take to get the meal on the table. The clock icon means you can get a feel for this at a flick through the book.

Most of the recipes in this book are easy, even (or perhaps especially) if they take a long time. Long cooking times can often mean a one-pot dinner bubbling on the stove or a roast cooking in the oven, both requiring minimal involvement from the chef. So don't be put off by long cooking times and check the recipe first.

Occasionally a recipe will specify additional time, such as for freezing or pickling. If so, this is indicated in words under the timer icon.

 The green carrot icon indicates a dish which is vegetarian.

 The red wheat icon indicates a dish which is gluten-free. As anyone avoiding it will know, gluten can pop up in the strangest of places, so if you are following a strict gluten-free diet be sure to check the ingredients label on any pre-packaged sauces or marinades. Keep a particular eye out for staple items such as baking powder, cornflour or soy sauce as these can contain gluten. If you are a coeliac, follow your usual dietary precautions.

 The red milk bottle icon indicates a recipe that is dairy-free. Eggs are not included in our definition of dairy-free, but all cows' milk–based products are. Substituting nut milks for dairy or coconut cream for cream are neat tricks for those learning to live on dairy-free diets, so if you'd like to try a recipe here that isn't dairy-free, you might be able to experiment with a few clever substitutions. Note that we have assumed in the recipes that store-bought pastries are dairy-free as these are generally made with vegetable oil not butter, but be sure to check ingredients carefully when purchasing.

kitchen staples

Along with the 6 or less key ingredients featured in each recipe, you may also need a few staples. Make sure that your fridge and pantry are well stocked with the following items.

Dry Goods

Flour
plain flour
self-raising flour

Sugar
white sugar
caster sugar
brown sugar

Cornflour

Bicarbonate of soda

Baking powder

From the Fridge

Butter

Milk

Eggs
(see note on page 8)

Seasonings

Oil
olive oil
vegetable oil
coconut oil

Vinegar
white wine vinegar
balsamic vinegar
red wine vinegar

Salt/sea salt

Fresh pepper

Vanilla essence/extract

greek

Greek Salad

2 stems cherry
tomatoes, halved

½ tsp dried oregano

1 red onion, sliced

½ cup (20g, ¾ oz)
basil leaves

½ cup (115g, 4oz)
Kalamata olives

200g (7oz) Greek
feta, thickly sliced

STAPLES

½ cup (125ml,
4fl oz) olive oil

OPTIONAL

2 Lebanese
cucumbers,
coarsely chopped

Combine the tomato, oregano, onion, olives
and half the oil in a serving bowl and toss
gently to combine.

Top with feta and basil, drizzle with
remaining oil, and serve immediately.

40 MIN

 4

Tzatziki

2 cucumbers

2 cups (500ml, 1pt)
Greek yoghurt

1 tsp fresh lemon
juice

1 medium clove
garlic, crushed

½ tbsp fresh dill,
finely chopped,
reserve a small
sprig for garnish

STAPLES

1 tsp extra virgin
olive oil

1 tsp salt

1 pinch freshly
ground pepper

1 tsp apple cider
vinegar

Peel, grate and then strain the cucumbers
to remove excess liquid.

Mix everything together in a bowl and stir
to thoroughly combine.

Season further to taste. Let sit for at least
30 minutes to let the flavours infuse.

Serve with a small amount of oil drizzled over
the top and garnished with a sprig of dill.

**55 MIN
+ RESTING**

Dolmades

½ onion, finely chopped

½ cup (80g, 3oz) long-grain rice

1 lemon, juiced and zested

¼ cup (10g, ¼ oz) mint, finely chopped

½ tsp dried oregano

40 canned grapevine leaves in brine, drained and rinsed

STAPLES

¼ cup (60ml, 2fl oz) plus 1 tbsp olive oil

1 cup (250ml, 8fl oz) water

½ tsp salt

OPTIONAL

Greek yoghurt, for dipping

Heat 1 tablespoon olive oil in a large saucepan over medium heat, add onion and saute for 5 minutes or until just tender. Add rice and stir to coat in oil. Add water and lemon juice, bring to a simmer, reduce heat to low, cover and cook for 5 minutes or until rice has absorbed all the liquid and is partly cooked. Stir in mint, oregano and salt. Set aside to cool slightly.

Working with one vine leaf at a time, place leaf on a work surface with the stem end pointing towards you. Place 2 teaspoons of rice mixture across the leaf near the stem end, in a cylinder shape. Fold stem end towards centre, then fold in the sides to enclose the rice. Roll up tightly like a cigar. Transfer to a large saucepan. Repeat with remaining vine leaves and filling, fitting dolmades snugly into the saucepan and leaving no gaps.

Drizzle dolmades with olive oil and invert a heavy plate over the top to weigh them down during cooking. Add enough water to just reach the plate. Cover with a lid and simmer over low heat for 30 minutes or until rice is cooked through and water has been absorbed.

Remove from heat and set aside for at least 30 minutes to develop flavours and cool slightly.

Serve warm or at room temperature with yoghurt for dipping.

10 MIN

Barbecued Calamari

600g (1lb 5oz)
(1lb 5oz) calamari
hoods, cleaned

½ tsp dried oregano

Juice of 1 lime, plus
extra lime wedges,
to garnish

STAPLES

2 tbsps olive oil

Salt, to taste

OPTIONAL

Parsley leaves,
to garnish

Pat calamari dry with paper towels to remove any surface
moisture.

Heat oil on a barbecue plate over high heat until smoking.
Add calamari and cook, turning often, for 1 minute or until just
cooked through.

Transfer to a serving plate and scatter with oregano.
Drizzle with lime juice and season to taste with salt. Serve
immediately, garnished with parsley if desired.

30 MIN

Zucchini Chips

2 zucchinis, thinly sliced

1 cup (125g, 4oz) breadcrumbs

½ cup (50g, 2oz) Parmesan cheese, grated

2 tsps paprika

STAPLES

2 eggs, beaten

¼ cup (60ml, 2fl oz) water

2 tbsps olive oil

½ cup (60g, 2oz) plain flour

½ tsp salt

½ tsp black pepper

OPTIONAL

Dipping sauce of choice

Preheat oven to 200°C (400°F, Gas Mark 6) and line a baking tray with greaseproof paper.

In a large mixing bowl combine the breadcrumbs and Parmesan. In a separate bowl combine the beaten egg with the water. In a third bowl combine the flour with paprika, salt and pepper.

Dip a zucchini slice in the flour mixture, then the egg mixture, then the breadcrumb mixture. Place the slice on the baking tray. Repeat until all the slices are on the baking tray in a single layer. Lightly drizzle them with oil.

Cook for 20 minutes or until golden and crispy, turning over halfway through.

Serve with dipping sauce.

Avgolemono

1 cup (210g, 7oz) orzo (or medium-grain rice)

4 large spring onions, white parts finely chopped

1 clove garlic, crushed

8 cups (2L, 4pt) chicken stock

2½ cups (315g, 11oz) cooked chicken, shredded

2 lemons; 1½ juiced, ½ thinly sliced for garnish

STAPLES

1 tbsp olive oil

2 eggs

1 tsp salt

Freshly ground pepper

OPTIONAL

Fresh chives, chopped, to garnish

Cook the orzo according to the packet directions, but reduce cooking time by 3 minutes, until still slightly firm. Drain and set aside.

Heat the oil in a large pot over medium heat. Fry the spring onions and garlic for 5 minutes until softened.

Add the stock and chicken and heat until boiling. Reduce the heat to low and scoop out 1 cup of stock.

Whisk the eggs and half the lemon juice together in a bowl. Slowly pour in the cup of stock, stirring continuously. Stir into the soup and add more lemon juice to taste.

Season with salt and pepper and serve garnished with chives and slices of lemon.

45 MIN

4

Lentil Soup

3 cloves garlic, crushed

2 small stalks celery, chopped

1 large onion, finely chopped

1 cup (185g, 6oz) green lentils, soaked overnight and drained

1 x 400g (14oz) can crushed tomatoes

8 cups (2L, 4pt) vegetable stock

STAPLES

1½ tbsps olive oil

2 cups (500ml, 1pt) water

2 tbsps red wine vinegar

1 tsp salt

Freshly ground pepper

OPTIONAL

Handful fresh basil leaves

½ cup (125ml, 4fl oz) Greek yoghurt

Heat the olive oil over medium heat in a large pot. Fry the garlic, celery and onion for 5 minutes until softened.

Add the lentils, tomatoes, stock and water and bring to a boil. Reduce the heat to a simmer and cook for 30 minutes or until the lentils are cooked.

Add the vinegar and salt and pepper to taste. Stir through fresh basil and serve with a dollop of yoghurt on top,. if using.

20 MIN

Fried Sardines

600g (1lb 5oz) small fresh sardines, cleaned, rinsed and patted dry

½ tsp ground oregano

1 cup (75g, 3oz) iceberg lettuce, shredded

1 lemon, cut into wedges, to serve

STAPLES

½ cup (75g, 3oz) cornflour

Freshly ground salt and pepper

2 large eggs

1 tbsp water

Olive oil, for frying

Mix the cornflour and oregano and a couple of grinds of salt and pepper, then spread out the mixture in a shallow dish.

Beat the eggs with the water and place in a separate shallow dish.

Lightly coat the sardines in the flour, shaking off any excess, then coat in the egg mixture, then coat in the flour again.

In a large, deep-sided frying pan, heat 1½ cm (¾ in) of oil until it shimmers. Fry the sardines in batches for 1 minute on each side until crispy and browned.

Drain on paper towels and serve them on a bed of lettuce with lemon wedges on the side.

Seafood and Rice

20 small mussels

1 small onion, chopped

2¼ cups (350g, 12oz) risotto rice (Arborio or carnaroli)

¼ cup (30g, 1oz) creme fraiche (or sour cream)

50g (2oz) calamari rings

20 large raw prawns, peeled

STAPLES

40g (2oz) unsalted butter

2 tbsps olive oil

4 cups (1L, 2pt) warm water (or use fish or vegetable stock)

Salt

Wash the mussels by scrubbing them clean and pulling out the beards. Heat about 2cm (1in) water in a large saucepan then place the mussels in the pan. Cover and cook for 3 minutes, stirring occasionally, until the mussels have opened. Strain the liquid through a sieve to remove any grit and reserve the liquid. Carefully remove the mussel flesh from all but eight of the shells and set the mussels aside.

To make the risotto, heat the butter and oil in a heavy-based frying pan over medium-high heat. Add the onion and cook for 4 minutes until softened. Add the rice and stir for 2 minutes until well coated with butter and slightly translucent.

Reduce the heat to medium. Add the 4 cups of water (or stock if preferred) to the rice, a cup at a time, stirring until all the liquid has been absorbed before adding the next portion. Season with salt to taste.

Once all the liquid is absorbed, check the rice. It should be tender but still slightly firm to the bite. If it hasn't reached this stage, add more water (or stock) as needed. Once the rice is al dente, stir through the creme fraiche. Cover and let it sit.

Lightly brush the rest of the seafood with olive oil and grill or fry for 3 minutes. Add the seafood immediately to the risotto and carefully fold it through.

25 MIN

Mediterranean Baked Trout

2 rainbow trout fillets

200g (7oz) cherry tomatoes, quartered

Juice of ½ lemon

2 tbsps fresh rosemary leaves

STAPLES

2 tbsps balsamic vinegar

1 tsp olive oil

Salt and pepper

OPTIONAL

½ lemon, cut into wedges, to serve

Preheat the oven to 200°C (400°F, Gas Mark 6).

Take two large pieces of baking paper and fold both in half.

Place the tomatoes on one side of each piece of paper.

Place a piece of fish over the top and then sprinkle over the lemon juice, rosemary leaves, balsamic vinegar and olive oil.

Fold the paper over the stacked tomatoes and fish. From the top corner, fold the edge over and crease with your fingernail. Continue to fold and crease all the way around until you have a sealed pocket.

Place on a rimmed baking tray and and bake in the oven for 15 minutes.

Serve with salt and pepper and a wedge of lemon.

45 MIN

Eggplant Dip

1 large eggplant

1 small onion,
quartered and
sliced

2 cloves garlic,
crushed

2 small red chillies,
seeded and finely
sliced

1 tsp ground
coriander

1 tsp ground cumin

STAPLES

2 tbsps olive oil

1 tsp salt

OPTIONAL

Crusty bread,
to serve

Grill eggplant over an open flame. When skin
begins to blacken place in a sealed plastic
bag for 15 minutes to sweat. Once cool, peel
off skin and roughly chop flesh.

Heat oil in a large frying pan over medium
heat. Add onion, garlic and chillies and
saute for 10 minutes, until onion is soft. Add
eggplant flesh and cook for 15 minutes, until
eggplant is breaking apart. Add salt and
spices and stir through for 2 more minutes.

Mash the mixture until it is a thick sauce
consistency. Season to taste and serve warm
with crusty bread

15 MIN
+ MARINATING

Garlic-Marinated Olives and Feta

500g (1lb) Greek feta, cubed

¾ cup (100g, 3½ oz) whole Kalamata olives

¾ cup (100g, 3½ oz) whole green olives

4 small cloves of garlic, sliced

2 tbsps fresh oregano, finely chopped

2 tbsps fresh sage leaves

STAPLES

½ tbsp freshly ground pepper

1 tsp salt

¾ cup (200ml, 7fl oz) extra virgin olive oil

2 tsps balsamic vinegar

OPTIONAL

1 tsp chilli flakes

2 tsps red onion, finely chopped

¾ cup (115g, 4oz) baby capsicums

½ tbsp lemon juice

Place the feta, olives, garlic, oregano, sage, pepper and salt, and if using, the chilli, onion and capsicums in a large bowl. Gently toss to coat but try not to break up the feta.

Place the mix into a sealable container and pour enough olive oil over the top to cover everything. Add the vinegar (and lemon juice if using).

Let the mixture marinate in the fridge overnight before serving.

Will keep for at least a week in the fridge.

40 MIN

Easy Spinach and Feta Triangles

2 bunches baby
spinach, trimmed,
washed and
shredded

100g (3½ oz) feta
cheese, crumbled

2 sheets frozen puff
pastry, just thawed,
quartered

STAPLES

2 tsps olive oil

2 eggs

Pepper

Preheat the oven to 200°C (390°F, Gas Mark 6) and line a large baking tray with greaseproof paper (use two trays if necessary).

Heat the oil in a large frying pan over a medium-high heat. Cook the spinach, while tossing, for 3 minutes or until it has wilted. Set aside to cool, then squeeze out any excess moisture and finely chop.

In a bowl lightly whisk one egg. Stir in the spinach and feta, and season with pepper.

Whisk the other egg. Divide the spinach filling among the pastry quarters and brush the edges with the egg. Fold in half diagonally, enclosing the filling and creating triangles. Pinch the edges to seal. Place the pastries on the prepared trays and bake for 20 minutes or until puffed and golden. Serve with any extra spinach leaves.

1 HR, 30 MIN

Spanakopita

1 large onion, finely chopped

500g (1lb) fresh baby spinach, finely chopped (can use frozen spinach)

2 tbsps fresh dill, finely chopped

250g (9oz) Greek feta

375g (13oz) filo pastry sheets

2 tbsps lemon zest

STAPLES

2 tbsps olive oil

3 large eggs, lightly beaten

Freshly ground pepper

2 tbsps unsalted butter, melted

2 tbsps plain flour

OPTIONAL

3 small cloves garlic, crushed

¼ tsp ground nutmeg

Preheat the oven to 180°C (350°F, Gas Mark 4) and lightly oil a large casserole dish

Heat the olive oil in a large saucepan over medium heat. Fry the onion (and garlic if using) for 4 minutes then add the spinach and dill. Cook for another 4 minutes or until the spinach is wilted. Drain excess liquid. Place the mixture into a large bowl and let it cool for 20 minutes.

Add the eggs, feta, zest, nutmeg (if using) and a couple of grinds of pepper to the spinach mixture. Mix to combine thoroughly.

Place one layer of filo pastry in the bottom of the dish and up the sides and lightly brush with melted butter. Place another layer on top and sides. Repeat two more times. Pour the spinach mixture into the dish. Place one layer of filo and lightly brush with butter. Repeat with another four sheets of pastry.

Bake for at least 45 minutes until the pastry is browned and the mixture is cooked through.

Let cool for 10 minutes before serving.

1 HR, 20 MIN

Feta Pie

15 sheets filo
pastry

75g (3oz) cream
cheese, room
temperature

100g (3½ oz) Greek
feta, crumbled

400g (14oz) fresh
ricotta

2 tbsps Greek
yoghurt

¼ tsp nutmeg

STAPLES

3 eggs, lightly
beaten

Salt and pepper

Preheat oven to 190°C (375°F, Gas Mark 5).
Lightly oil a 23 x 4cm (9 x 1½in) pie dish.

In a large bowl, thoroughly mix together the
cheeses, eggs, yoghurt and nutmeg.

Lay out one sheet of pastry (keep the rest
in the packet so it doesn't dry out). Place a
portion of the mixture along the long edge
of the pastry, about 3cm (1in) wide.

Starting at the end with the mixture, gently
roll the pastry up into a tube. Place the tube
along the edge of the pie dish.

Repeat with the second filo sheet. Keep
placing the tubes in the dish so that they
form a coil. Continue until you have filled
the dish with the coiled tubes.

Sprinkle with water and brush with olive oil.
Bake for 50 minutes, until golden brown.

25 MIN

4

Asparagus and Goat's Cheese Tartlets

16 shortcrust pastry tartlet cases, store bought

1 bunch asparagus, ends trimmed

2 cloves garlic, minced

⅔ cup (160ml, 5fl oz) single cream

150g (5oz) goat's cheese

STAPLES

10g (¼ oz) butter

2 eggs, beaten

Salt and pepper

Preheat the oven to 180°C (350°F, Gas Mark 4) and lay out the tartlet cases on a baking tray (or two) lined with greaseproof paper. Cut the asparagus spears in half. Finely chop the bottom halves. Slice the top halves in half lengthways and set aside.

In a frying pan over a medium heat, melt the butter and add the chopped asparagus and garlic. Cook, stirring occasionally, for about 5 minutes or until soft. Distribute the cooked asparagus and goat's cheese among the cases.

Combine the egg and cream in a bowl. Mix well, season with salt and pepper then pour this over the asparagus and cheese in the cases. Place two halves of asparagus tip on each tartlet.

Cook in the oven for 15 minutes or until slightly browned.

1 HR

Rice and Ricotta Pie

2 cups (450g, 1lb)
cooked brown rice

3 tbsps Parmesan
cheese, grated

1 large onion, finely
chopped

500g (1lb) fresh
ricotta cheese

½ cup (60g, 2oz)
Cheddar cheese,
grated

1 cup (30g, 1oz)
fresh spinach, finely
chopped

STAPLES

1 tsp plus 2 tbsps
olive oil

3 eggs, lightly
beaten

½ tsp pepper

¼ tsp salt

Preheat oven to 190°C (375°F, Gas Mark 5).

Lightly grease a 25cm (2in) (10in) pie dish
with 1 teaspoon olive oil. In a medium bowl,
mix together the rice and Parmesan. Press
the mix into the pie dish and about 2cm (1in)
up the sides. If the mixture becomes too
sticky, dip your fingers in some water.

In a large bowl, thoroughly mix the onion,
ricotta, Cheddar, spinach, eggs, pepper and
salt. Place onto the rice base and cook for
45 minutes or until the edges are browned
and the filling is set in the middle.

15 MIN

 4

Crunchy Bean and Feta Salad

600g (1lb 5oz) fresh green beans

300g (10oz) Greek feta, cubed

Lemon wedges, to serve

STAPLES

¼ cup (60ml, 2fl oz) olive oil

Freshly ground pepper

Salt

Trim the ends of the beans and cut into 4cm (1½ in) lengths.

Bring a large pot of lightly salted water to the boil. Add the beans and boil for 1 minute then drain and rinse under cold water.

Place the beans and feta in a large bowl. Drizzle the oil over the top and give it a good couple of grinds of pepper.

Gently toss to coat the beans and feta with the oil. Season to taste with salt and pepper and serve with lemon wedges on the side.

20 MIN

 4

Traditional Baked Feta

2 x 200g (7oz) blocks Greek feta

¼ cup (35g, 1¼ oz) Kalamata olives, pitted and sliced

1 small red onion, quartered and finely sliced

2 tbsps fresh oregano, finely chopped

½ cup (10g, ¼ oz) basil leaves

3 medium Roma tomatoes, quartered and sliced

STAPLES

⅓ cup (75ml, 2½ fl oz) olive oil

OPTIONAL

1 lemon, cut into wedges, to serve

Preheat the oven to 200°C (400°F, Gas Mark 6).

Slice each block of feta in half through the shortest edge so you have four flat rectangles.

Lay out four sheets of foil, large enough to completely enclose each rectangle of feta.

Place a piece of feta in the centre of each piece of foil. Top each slice with equal portions of olives, onion, oregano, basil and tomato.

Drizzle 1 tablespoon of oil over each. Wrap up each square, place them on a baking tray and bake for 12 minutes until heated through.

Serve hot with lemon wedges on the side.

Prawns with Tomato and Feta

750g (1½ lb) prawn tails, cleaned, shelled and patted dry

1 red onion, finely chopped

8 Roma tomatoes, chopped

400g (14oz) Greek feta

1 tsp ground fennel seeds

¾ cup (35g, 1¼ oz) fresh parsley, finely chopped

STAPLES

3 tbsps olive oil

1½ tbsps red wine vinegar

Freshly ground salt and pepper

OPTIONAL

2 large cloves garlic, crushed

⅓ cup (80ml, 3fl oz) Greek ouzo (or white wine)

Heat the oil in a deep-sided frying pan over medium heat. Fry the onion (and garlic if using) for 5 minutes until the onion is softened. Add the tomatoes, fennel and vinegar and cook for another 5 minutes until the tomatoes have softened. Bring to a boil then pour in the ouzo or wine, if using, and cook for 1 minute.

Reduce the heat to a simmer, add the prawns and cook for 5 minutes or until they're cooked through.

Season the mixture to taste. Serve the prawns with the feta crumbled over the top and sprinkled with parsley.

20 MIN
+ MARINATING

Lemon Chicken Kebabs

800g (1¾ lb) chicken breast fillet, cut into bite-size chunks

1 large lemon; ½ juiced, ½ cut into slices

3 small cloves garlic, crushed

2 tsps ground oregano

½ tsp chilli powder

1 cup (260g, 9oz) tzatziki (shop-bought or see recipe page 15)

12 wooden skewers, soaked in hot water for at least 30 minutes

STAPLES

⅓ cup (80ml, 3fl oz) olive oil

Freshly ground salt and pepper

Place the chicken pieces in a large bowl. Add the lemon juice, garlic, oregano, chilli powder, olive oil and a couple of grinds of salt and pepper. Toss to combine, then let the chicken marinate for at least 2 hours, covered, in the refrigerator.

Heat a grill plate to medium-high heat.

Thread the chicken pieces onto the skewers.

Grill the skewers for 8 minutes, turning every 2 minutes, or until cooked through.

Serve the skewers hot, garnished with lemon slices and tzatziki sauce on the side.

4

Chicken and Chips Souvlaki

3 large floury potatoes, cut into thick chips, patted dry

750g (1½ lb) chicken thigh fillets, cut into thirds

3 cloves garlic, crushed

½ tbsp ground oregano

4 souvlaki pides

1 cup (260g, 9oz) tzatziki (shop-bought or see recipe page 15)

STAPLES

½ cup (120ml, 4fl oz) olive oil

2 tsps salt

1 tsp pepper

OPTIONAL

½ tbsp dried rosemary leaves, chopped

3 Roma tomatoes, halved and sliced

1 medium red onion, halved and thinly sliced

Preheat oven to 180°C (350°F, Gas Mark 4). Toss the chips with 1 tablespoon oil, half the salt and the rosemary, if using. Spread over a flat baking tray and bake for 40 minutes until browned, turning every 15 minutes.

Toss the chicken with the garlic, oregano, ⅓ cup oil and the remaining salt and pepper. Marinate in the fridge for at least 2 hours.

Heat a grill to medium-high heat and grill the chicken pieces for 5 minutes on each side or until cooked through. Brush the remaining oil over the pides and grill them for 1 minute on each side.

Cut the chicken into bite-size pieces and place on the pides with the chips, tomato, onion and dollops of tzatziki.

4

Moussaka

3 cups (375g, 13oz) mozzarella, grated

1 large onion, finely chopped

800g (1¾ lb) minced lamb

¼ tsp nutmeg

1 x 400g (14oz) crushed tomatoes

2 large eggplants, cut into 1cm (½ in) thick slices

STAPLES

1 tbsp butter

1 heaped tbsp plain flour

1 cup (250ml, 8fl oz) milk

Freshly ground salt and pepper

2 tbsps olive oil

OPTIONAL

3 small cloves garlic, crushed

Fresh rosemary leaves, to garnish

Preheat the oven to 180°C (350°F, Gas Mark 4).

In small saucepan, melt the butter over medium heat until just starting to foam. Add the flour and cook for 1 minute, stirring. Add the milk a small amount at a time, stirring continuously for 5 minutes until you have a smooth thick sauce. Once it starts to boil, stir in ½ cup of mozzarella and season to taste with salt. Remove from heat, cover and set aside.

Heat the oil in a large frying pan over medium-high heat. Fry the onion (and garlic, if using) for 4 minutes. Add the lamb and nutmeg and fry for 8 minutes or until the lamb is browned.

Add the tomatoes and stir through. Season the mixture to taste.

Place half the lamb mixture into the bottom of a casserole dish and half the eggplant slices over the top. Pour half the cheese sauce over the top and sprinkle half the remaining mozzarella over the top. Repeat with the rest of the lamb, eggplant, sauce and mozzarella.

Bake for 40 minutes or until the cheese is golden. Let stand for 10 minutes before serving. Garnish with fresh rosemary leaves.

3 HR, 30 MIN

Lamb Shanks with Feta and Eggplant

2 eggplants, cut into 1cm (½ in) thick slices

2 tbsps lemon zest

1 tbsp ground oregano

4 lamb shanks

2½ cups (630g, 1lb 6oz) crushed tomatoes

300g (10oz) Greek feta, cubed

STAPLES

⅓ cup (80ml, 3fl oz) olive oil

Freshly ground salt and pepper

1 tbsp balsamic vinegar

OPTIONAL

4 small cloves garlic, crushed

Preheat oven to 220°C (425°F, Gas Mark 7).

Layer the eggplant slices in the bottom of a large baking dish. Sprinkle over the zest and oregano (and garlic, if using).

Heat ½ tablespoon oil in a large frying pan over medium-high heat. Sear the lamb shanks all over in the pan. Place the shanks on top of the eggplant. Pour the tomatoes over the top of the shanks and sprinkle a couple of good grinds of salt and pepper over the top along with the rest of the oil, vinegar and thyme. Cover with a lid or foil and roast for 20 minutes.

Turn the heat down to 160°C (325°F, Gas Mark 3). Remove the dish from the oven, turn the shanks over and ladle some of the liquid from the dish over the top. Return to the oven, covered, for at least 3 hours, turning the shanks every hour until the meat is tender.

Serve the shanks with the feta on the side.

2 HR, 30 MIN

Stufado

800g (1¾ lb) sirloin steak, cut into 2½ cm (1in) cubes

10 small shallots, peeled

3 small cloves garlic, crushed

¾ cup (175ml, 6fl oz) red wine

2 x 400g (14oz) can crushed tomatoes; 1 can pureed until smooth

1½ tsps allspice

STAPLES

2 tbsps olive oil

2 tbsps white wine vinegar

Freshly ground salt and pepper

Heat the oil in a large heavy-bottomed pot over medium-high heat. Brown the meat in batches, then set aside.

Reduce the heat to medium, add the shallots, garlic and more oil if needed and cook until softened for 8 minutes.

Add the wine and vinegar and simmer for 2 minutes, scraping off any bits from the bottom of the pot.

Return the meat to the pot with the tomatoes, pureed tomatoes and allspice. Bring to a boil, then reduce the heat to low, cover and simmer for 2 hours. Add water if needed while cooking if it looks like drying out.

Once the beef is tender, season to taste and serve hot.

30 MIN
+ MARINATING

Lime and Thyme Souvlaki Skewers

800g (1¾ lb) lamb steaks, cut into 1½ cm (¾ in) cubes

½ tsp ground oregano

1½ tbsps thyme leaves

3 small cloves garlic, crushed

⅓ cup (75ml, 2½ fl oz) fresh lime juice

12 wooden skewers, soaked in hot water for at least 30 minutes

STAPLES

3 tbsps olive oil

Freshly ground salt and pepper

OPTIONAL

1 batch freshly baked chips (see recipe page 43)

Toss the lamb together with the oregano, thyme, garlic, lime juice and olive oil along with a couple of good grinds of salt and pepper, then marinate, covered, for at least 1 hour in the refrigerator.

Thread the cubes onto the skewers.

Heat a grill plate to high heat and cook the lamb for 8 minutes or until cooked through, turning the skewers every 2 minutes. Drizzle over leftover marinade to keep the lamb moist.

Serve the skewers with hot chips, if desired.

**30 MIN
+ MARINATING**

Thyme-Marinated Pork with Tomato and Bean Salad

¼ cup (10g, ¼ oz) thyme leaves, finely chopped

4 x 200g (7oz) pork steaks

600g (1lb 5oz) green beans, ends trimmed

5 large tomatoes

1 small red onion, finely chopped

½ cup (20g, ¾ oz) fresh parsley, chopped

STAPLES

½ cup (120ml, 4fl oz) olive oil

Freshly ground salt and pepper

¼ cup (50ml, 2fl oz) red wine vinegar

Mix together half the olive oil, the thyme and a couple of grinds of salt and pepper. Coat the steaks in the herb oil and let them marinate, covered, in the refrigerator for at least 2 hours. Then remove them from the refrigerator and let them come to room temperature before cooking.

Bring a large pot of lightly salted water to the boil. Add the beans and boil them for 1 ½ minutes, then immediately drain and rinse them under cold water and set aside.

Chop the tomatoes and toss together with the onion and parsley in a large bowl. Mix together the rest of the oil with the vinegar and a couple of grinds of salt and pepper. Pour over the tomatoes and again toss to combine.

Heat a grill to medium-high heat. Grill the steaks for 6 minutes on each side until cooked through, basting with leftover marinade. Let the steaks sit for 5 minutes before serving.

Serve the steaks with the beans and salad.

40 MIN

Lamb Meatballs with Couscous

600g (1lb 5oz) minced lamb

3 small cloves garlic, crushed

3 spring onions, white parts finely minced, green ends sliced

½ tbsps ground oregano

1 large lemon; ½ zested, ½ cut into wedges

2 cups (380g, 14oz) couscous

STAPLES

3 tbsps olive oil

2 cups (500ml, 1pt) boiling water

Freshly ground salt and pepper

OPTIONAL

½ tsp ground chilli

Cucumber and olive salad, to serve

Place the lamb, garlic, minced spring onion, oregano, lemon zest and chilli, if using, in a bowl and mix thoroughly. Form the mixture into small 2½ cm (1in) balls.

Place the couscous in a large heatproof bowl. Pour over the boiling water. Stir through, cover and let sit for at least 7 minutes. Drizzle 1 tablespoon of oil over the top and fluff up with a fork. Season to taste and set aside.

Heat the rest of the oil in a large frying pan. Cook the meatballs for 10 minutes, turning every 2 minutes until cooked through.

Serve the meatballs on top of the couscous, sprinkled with the sliced spring onions and with lemon wedges on the side. Serve with cucumber and olive salad, if desired.

Chicken and Kalamata Olive Stew

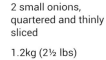

2 small onions, quartered and thinly sliced

1.2kg (2½ lbs) chicken pieces, skin on

2 small red capsicums, deseeded and cut into thick slices

2 x 400g (14oz) cans chopped tomatoes

2 bay leaves

2 cups (280g, 10oz) Kalamata olives, pitted

STAPLES

2 tbsps olive oil

½ cup (125ml, 4fl oz) water (or use dry white wine)

2 tbsps red wine vinegar

Freshly ground salt and pepper

OPTIONAL

3 small cloves garlic, crushed

2 tbsps dried oregano leaves

Heat the oil in a large pot over medium heat. Fry the onions (and garlic, if using) for 4 minutes until softened. Add the chicken in batches and brown, then remove from the pan.

Pour in the water and scrape any bits from the bottom of the pot for 1 minute. Add the capsicum, tomatoes, bay leaves and vinegar (and oregano, if using). Heat until it starts to boil. Reduce the heat to low and simmer for 8 minutes.

Return the chicken to the pot and add the olives. Cover and simmer for 35 minutes until the chicken is tender.

Season to taste and serve hot.

Slow-Roasted Lamb Gyros

1.2kg (2½ lbs) boneless leg of lamb

6 large cloves garlic, crushed

⅓ cup (100ml, 3½ fl oz) lemon juice

3 tbsps fresh rosemary, chopped

1 tbsps ground oregano

6 souvlaki pides

STAPLES

1 tbsp salt

2 tsps freshly ground pepper

¾ cup (185ml, 6fl oz) olive oil

OPTIONAL

1 cup (260g, 9oz) tzatziki sauce (shop-bought or see recipe page 15)

Cucumber and tomato salad, to serve

Place the lamb in a large sealable bag and add the garlic, lemon juice, rosemary, oregano, salt, pepper and ½ cup olive oil. Seal the bag, pressing out the air. Massage the mixture into the lamb then marinate in the refrigerator for at least 24 hours.

Preheat the oven to 150°C (300°F, Gas Mark 2). Place the lamb and marinade in a roasting dish. Roast for 4 hours, along with a small water-filled bowl, basting regularly and ensuring there is always water in the bowl.

Slice lamb into bite-size chunks. Heat a grill plate to high heat and grill in batches, drizzling over the remaining oil until the lamb is slightly charred.

Serve the lamb in pides with tzatziki and salad.

45 MIN
+ DRAINING

Eggplant and Olive Gratin

3 large eggplants, ends trimmed, cut into 1cm (½ in) thick rounds

3 cups (680g, 1½ lb) tomato passata

1 cup (140g, 5oz) Kalamata olives, pitted and chopped

3 large cloves garlic, crushed

¼ cup (10g, ¼ oz) fresh thyme leaves

3 cups (375g, 13oz) mozzarella, grated

STAPLES

4 tbsps salt

¼ cup (50ml, 2fl oz) olive oil

1½ tbsps balsamic vinegar

Freshly ground salt and pepper

Layer the eggplants in a colander and sprinkle each layer with the salt. If time allows, let sit for 30 minutes. Drain the liquid and pat the slices dry.

Preheat oven to 220°C (425°F, Gas Mark 7).

Heat the olive oil in a large pot and add the tomato passata, olives, garlic and thyme. Heat until simmering, then stir in the vinegar and simmer for 5 minutes. Remove from the heat and set aside.

Layer the eggplant rounds in a casserole dish. Over each layer spoon a portion of the tomato sauce, then sprinkle over some mozzarella. Repeat these three layers.

Bake in the oven for 30 minutes or until the eggplant is softened and cooked through. Season to taste and serve.

Juicy Bifteki Burgers

500g (1lb) minced beef

1 small onion, grated and squeezed to remove excess liquid

2 large cloves garlic, crushed

1½ tsps ground oregano

½ cup (60g, 2oz) breadcrumbs

200g (7oz) Greek feta, cut into 4 cubes

STAPLES

1 egg, lightly beaten

Freshly ground salt and pepper

1½ tbsps olive oil

OPTIONAL

Lemon wedges, to serve

Greek salad, to serve (see recipe page 14)

Place the mince, onion, garlic, oregano, breadcrumbs, egg and a couple of grinds of salt and pepper in a large bowl and mix thoroughly.

Divide into four equal amounts and form into balls. Press a piece of feta into the centre of each ball and reform into slightly flattened patties.

Heat a grill pan to medium-high heat. Brush each patty with oil and grill for 7 minutes on each side until cooked through.

Serve the patties with a Greek salad on the side and with lemon wedges.

10 HR, 30 MIN

Slow Cooker Lamb Kleftiko

1.2kg (2½ lbs) lamb shoulder

8 medium waxy potatoes, halved (use Bintje or Kipfler)

6 cloves garlic, crushed

2 tbsps ground oregano

½ cup (125ml, 4fl oz) dry white wine

1 large lemon; ½ juiced, ½ cut into slices

STAPLES

¼ cup (50ml, 2fl oz) olive oil

1 tbsp salt

Freshly ground pepper

OPTIONAL

2 bay leaves

2 cups (280g, 10oz) black olives, pitted

Fresh parsley leaves, to garnish

1 large stalk celery, sliced, to garnish

Mix together the oil, garlic, oregano, salt and a couple of grinds of pepper. Rub into the lamb shoulder.

Layer the lemon slices on the bottom of the cooker and place the lamb on top.

Pour the wine and lemon juice around the lamb and add the bay leaves, if using. Sit the potato halves around the lamb.

Set the slow cooker to low and let it cook, covered, for 10 hours. Add the olives, if using, after 6 hours.

Once the meat and potatoes are tender, remove from the cooker, spoon over the juices and serve garnished with parsley and celery.

1 HR, 15 MIN

Roast Vegetable, Lentil and Feta Salad

1 cup (185g, 6oz) brown lentils

3 beetroots, peeled and cut into 3cm (1in) chunks

2 carrots, halved lengthways and cut on the diagonal into 2cm (1in) thick slices

Seeds from 1 large pomegranate

250g (9oz) Greek feta

¼ cup (60ml, 2fl oz) lemon juice

STAPLES

⅓ cup (75ml, 2½ fl oz) olive oil

Freshly ground salt and pepper

OPTIONAL

Fresh parsley leaves, to garnish

Rinse the lentils then add to a pot of lightly salted water.

Bring to a boil, then reduce the heat to a gentle simmer for 20 minutes. Add water as needed. Once the lentils are tender, strain and set aside to cool.

Preheat oven to 190°C (375°F, Gas Mark 5) and line a large flat baking tray with baking paper.

Toss the beetroot and carrot with half the olive oil and a couple of grinds of salt and pepper. Scatter in one layer over the baking tray.

Roast for 40 minutes until the vegetables are tender.

Place in a large bowl with the lentils, pomegranate seeds and crumbled feta. Drizzle the lemon juice and remaining oil over the top. Gently toss to combine, season to taste and serve garnished with parsley.

1 HR, 15 MIN

Greek Walnut Cake

2½ cups (310g, 10oz) walnuts, roughly chopped

2 tsps allspice

¾ tsp ground cloves

¾ cup (200ml, 7fl oz) Greek yoghurt

2 oranges; 1 zested and both juiced

1 tbsp cinnamon

STAPLES

130g (4oz) butter, room temperature

½ cup (80g, 3oz) dark brown sugar

¼ cup (55g, 2oz) caster sugar

2 eggs, separated

2 cups (250g, 8oz) self-raising flour

Preheat oven to 180°C (350°F, Gas Mark 4); grease and line a 20cm (8in) square cake tin.

Beat butter, brown sugar and caster sugar together until creamy. Add the egg yolks, one at a time, then mix through the flour, 1¾ cups walnuts, allspice, cinnamon and cloves.

Beat the egg whites until firm peaks form. Then beat through the yoghurt with 2 tsps of zest and ⅓ cup of orange juice. Add to the rest of the cake batter and stir through then pour into the cake tin. Bake for 45 minutes. Turn the cake out onto a wire rack to cool.

Place water, ⅓ cup orange juice, remaining sugar, cloves and cinnamon in a small saucepan over medium-high heat. Simmer, stirring, for 4 minutes until thickened.

Drizzle the syrup over the cake and sprinkle with walnuts to serve.

Revani

1 tsp ground cinnamon

1 large orange, zested and juiced

5 eggs, room temperature

1¼ cups (220g, 8oz) fine semolina

1½ cups (185g, 6oz) blanched almonds, finely chopped, plus 10 whole almonds

2 tbsps cognac (or brandy)

STAPLES

2½ cups (550g, 1lb, 4oz) caster sugar

3 cups (750ml, 24fl oz) water

200g (7oz) butter, room temperature

⅔ cup (80g, 3oz) plain flour

½ tbsp baking powder

1½ tsps vanilla essence

Stir together 1 ⅓ cups of sugar with the water in a pan over medium heat until just simmering. Stir in the cinnamon and orange zest over low heat for 12 minutes. Then turn off the heat and let the syrup cool.

Preheat oven to 180°C (350°F, Gas Mark 4) and line and grease a 25cm (10in) cake tin.

Beat together remaining sugar and butter until creamy. Beat in the eggs, one at a time, then the flour and semolina until completely combined. Finally beat in ¼ cup orange juice. Stir through chopped almonds, vanilla and cognac. Pour into the cake tin. Bake for 35 minutes.

Turn the cake out onto a wire rack to cool. Spoon the syrup over the top. Cut into pieces and finish with an almond on top.

italian

4 HR, 15 MIN

Slow-Roasted Tomatoes

500g (1lb) ripe
Roma tomatoes

3 tsps oregano,
finely chopped

4 basil leaves,
shredded

1 clove garlic,
minced

STAPLES

1½ tbsps salt

½ cup (125ml,
4fl oz) olive oil

Preheat oven to 110°C (230°F, Gas Mark ¼).
Line a large flat baking tray with foil.

Cut each tomato in thirds lengthwise. Lay
them out on the tray, cut sides up. Sprinkle a
very small amount of salt over the cut sides
of the tomatoes. Sprinkle over the oregano
as well. Slow cook the tomatoes for at least
4 hours, until the tomatoes have shrivelled
and are slightly dry. They should have lost
nearly all their water.

Place the tomatoes in a dry, clean jar with
the basil and garlic. Pour in enough olive oil
to completely cover the tomatoes. Store in
the fridge for a couple of weeks.

**25 MIN
+ COOLING**

CUPS

Ricotta Cheese

4 cups (1L, 2pt) full
cream milk

4 tbsps lemon juice
(about 2 lemons; or
use distilled white
vinegar)

STAPLES

½ tsp salt

In a large saucepan, bring the milk to a
near boil. Use a cooking thermometer
to make sure it doesn't get hotter than
85°C (185°F). As soon as you see bubbles
forming, remove the saucepan from the
heat. Don't let it simmer.

Add lemon juice and salt and stir gently.
Take time and allow the mixture to start to
curdle. Curdling happens when the liquid
and solids start to separate. The frothy
white solids will emerge from the liquid.

Allow it to cool for at least 1 hour to room
temperature.

Set up a fine-mesh colander over a large
bowl, then drape the colander with a damp
tea towel or layer of cheesecloth. Pour the
mixture through. Press the jelly-like curds
(the ricotta) lightly to drain away as much
of the liquid (whey) as possible.

Store ricotta in an airtight container in the
fridge for up to 5 days.

Peposo

1.5kg (3lb 5oz) stewing steak (or beef cheek, trimmed), cut into 2cm (1in) chunks

1 large onion, finely chopped

1¼ cups (300ml, 10fl oz) Pinot Noir

2 cups (500ml, 1pt) beef stock

1¼ cups (280g, 10oz) diced tomatoes

3 anchovy fillets, drained

STAPLES

3 tbsps cornflour

Freshly ground salt and pepper

⅓ cup (75ml, 2½ fl oz) olive oil

2 tbsps black peppercorns

OPTIONAL

2 tbsps juniper berries

3 large cloves garlic, crushed

Mix together the cornflour and a few grinds of salt and pepper in a large bowl. Add the beef and toss to lightly coat.

Heat the oil in a large heavy-based pot over medium-high heat. Add the onion (and garlic, if using) and then fry the beef in batches until browned and remove from the pan.

Reduce the heat to medium, add a splash of wine and the anchovies and stir for 1 minute. Return the beef, add half the wine and bring to a boil for 2 minutes, scraping any bits from the bottom of the pot. Add the stock and tomatoes (and juniper berries, if using) and bring to the boil. Reduce to low, then cover and simmer for at least 2½ hours until the beef is nearly falling apart.

Remove the lid and stir through the rest of the wine. Simmer for another 30 minutes until the sauce has thickened. Season to taste and serve.

30 MIN

Chicken Saltimbocca

4 x 150g (5oz) chicken breast fillets

8 slices prosciutto

16 sage leaves

¾ cup (180ml, 6fl oz) chicken stock

2 small lemons; 1 juiced, 1 cut into wedges

6 cups (180g, 6oz) mixed salad leaves

Toothpicks

STAPLES

⅓ cup (75ml, 2½ fl oz) olive oil

¾ tsp cornflour

Freshly ground salt and pepper

Place the chicken between two sheets of baking paper and flatten with a meat mallet until they're even thickness. Wrap the chicken fillets in the slices of prosciutto, placing sage leaves on the chicken and prosciutto as you wrap. Place one leaf on top and secure it and the prosciutto in place with a toothpick.

Heat the oil in a deep-sided frying pan over medium-high heat. Add the chicken and cook for 4 minutes on each side. Remove from the pan and set aside, covered.

Mix together the stock, 1 tablespoon lemon juice and cornflour then add to the pan over low heat and stir for 3 minutes until the sauce has thickened. Season to taste.

Serve the chicken on a bed of salad leaves with the sauce drizzled over.

2 HR, 30 MIN

Osso Bucco

6 osso bucco (about 1.2kg/2½ lbs)

2 small onions, chopped

1 x 400g (14oz) can crushed tomatoes

2 large carrots, chopped

3 small cloves garlic, crushed

1⅔ cups (400ml, 13fl oz) beef stock

STAPLES

4 tbsps plain flour

Freshly ground salt and pepper

2 tbsps olive oil

1 tbsp balsamic vinegar

OPTIONAL

½ tbsp ground oregano

Mashed potato, to serve

Preheat oven to 160°C (325°F, Gas Mark 3).

Mix together the flour and a few grinds of salt and pepper in a large bowl. Add the meat and toss to lightly coat.

Heat the oil in a large frying pan over medium heat. Add the onion, carrot and garlic and fry for 5 minutes. Add the meat and fry in batches until browned then place in an oven-proof casserole dish.

Pour a quarter of the stock into the pan and bring to a boil for 2 minutes, scraping off any bits from the bottom. Add the tomatoes, vinegar, oregano, if using, and the rest of the stock and bring to a boil.

Add the mix to the meat and bake in the oven for 2 hours. Serve with a side of mashed potato.

2 HR, 20 MIN
+ RESTING

 4

Slow Cooker
Ciabatta

3 cups (435g, 14oz)
bread flour

1¼ tsps instant
yeast

STAPLES

2 tbsps olive oil

1½ tsps salt

1½ cups (375ml,
13fl oz) warm water

1 tsp sugar

In a large bowl, combine the flour, yeast, oil
and salt. Stir with a whisk then slowly pour in
the water. Use your hands to mix together
into a ball.

Cover with plastic wrap and let it rest for at
least 6 hours, preferably overnight.

Line the slow cooker with baking paper.

Turn out the dough onto a lightly floured
surface and knead for 10 minutes. Sprinkle
the sugar into it as you need, spreading it
through the dough. Shape it into an oval and
place in the cooker.

Fit some paper towels snugly into the lid to
help absorb moisture and keep the crust as
dry as possible. Cook on high for 2 hours
until the bread is cooked through.

If you want to crisp up the crust, place it
under an oven grill on high for 5 minutes.

Serve with side accompaniments such as
sundried tomatoes and olive oil.

Zuppa Imperiale

5 slices Vienna bread, one day old

6 cups (1.5L, 50fl oz) chicken stock

½ cup (20g, ¾ oz) parsley, roughly chopped

1 pinch nutmeg

STAPLES

50g (2oz) butter

Freshly ground pepper

1 pinch of salt

Cut the bread into 2cm (1in) cubes.

Heat the butter in a medium-sized frying pan over medium-high heat. and fry the bread cubes in the butter for 3 minutes until slightly browned. Remove from the pan and set aside.

Bring the stock to a boil. Add the parsley and nutmeg, plus the salt and a couple of grinds of pepper. Let simmer for 10 minutes.

Serve with the bread cubes divided evenly between the soup bowls. Season to taste.

50 MIN

4

Simple Meatballs and Tomato Sauce

800g (1¾ lb) minced pork

1 cup (250ml, 8fl oz) beef stock

¾ cup (90g, 3oz) fresh breadcrumbs

2 cups (450g, 1lb) diced tomatoes

3 small cloves garlic, crushed

2 small onions; 1 grated and squeezed to remove excess liquid, 1 thickly sliced

STAPLES

2 tbsps olive oil

Freshly ground salt and pepper

1 small egg, lightly beaten

OPTIONAL

Freshly cooked pasta, to serve

Heat 2 teaspoons oil in a large deep-sided frying pan over medium heat and fry the garlic and grated onion for 1 minute. Remove from heat and place in a large mixing bowl.

Add the meat, breadcrumbs, 2 tablespoons of the stock, a couple of grinds of salt and pepper and the egg to the bowl and mix. Form into 2½ cm (1in) balls.

Heat the pan to medium-high and fry the meatballs in batches for 5 minutes, turning constantly until cooked through. Set aside, covered, in a warm place.

Add the rest of the oil to the pan over medium heat and fry the sliced onion for 4 minutes. Add the tomatoes, the rest of the stock and a couple of grinds of salt and pepper.

Bring to the boil, then reduce to low and simmer. Return the meatballs to the pan and simmer for 25 minutes. Season to taste and serve with freshly cooked pasta.

40 MIN

Spaghetti with Vegan Bolognaise

1½ large onions, finely chopped

500g (1lb) mushrooms, finely chopped

1 large carrot, finely chopped

1 large eggplant, chopped

2 x 400g (14oz) cans diced tomatoes

500g (1lb) spaghetti

STAPLES

2 tbsps olive oil

2 tbsps balsamic vinegar

½ tsp sugar

½ cup (125ml, 4fl oz) water

Freshly ground salt and pepper

OPTIONAL

1½ tbsps dried mixed herbs

¾ cup (75g, 3oz) grated vegan Parmesan

Sprigs fresh oregano, to garnish

Heat the oil in a large frying pan over medium heat. Fry the onion for 5 minutes until softened. Add the mushrooms and fry them for 2 more minutes.

Add the carrot and eggplant and fry for 5 more minutes until the carrot is slightly softened.

Turn the heat up to high, add the tomatoes, mixed herbs, if using, vinegar, sugar and water. Bring to a boil, then reduce the heat to low and simmer, covered, for 20 minutes. Add more water as needed.

Cook the spaghetti according to the packet directions and drain. Add to the sauce, season to taste and stir through for 1 minute.

Serve topped with vegan Parmesan and sprigs of oregano, if desired.

1 HR

Classic Bolognaise

1 large onion, finely chopped

400g (14oz) minced beef

2 small stalks celery, finely chopped

1 small carrot, finely chopped

1 x 400g (14oz) can crushed tomatoes

500g (1lb) linguini

STAPLES

2 tbsps olive oil

⅓ cup (90ml, 3fl oz) water

2 tsps balsamic vinegar

Freshly ground salt and pepper

OPTIONAL

¾ cup (75g, 3oz) grated Parmesan

Heat the oil in a large frying pan over medium heat. Fry the onion for 5 minutes until softened. Add the meat and fry for 5 minutes until browned.

Add the celery and carrot and fry for another 5 minutes. Increase the heat to high and add the tomatoes, water and vinegar and bring to a boil, stirring occasionally.

Reduce the heat to low and simmer the sauce, covered, for 30 minutes, adding more water as needed.

Cook the linguini according to the packet directions and drain. Add to the sauce, season to taste and stir through for 1 minute.

Serve topped with Parmesan.

Chicken, Mushroom and Tomato Tagliatelle

600g (1lb 5oz) chicken breast, cut into bite-size chunks

300g (10oz) button mushrooms, sliced

1 cup (250g, 9oz) cherry tomatoes, halved

½ cup (120ml, 4fl oz) white wine or chicken stock

1 tbsp dried basil

500g (1lb) tagliatelle

STAPLES

2 tbsps olive oil

1 tsp red wine vinegar

Freshly ground salt and pepper

OPTIONAL

2 large cloves garlic, crushed

Fresh basil leaves, to garnish

Heat the oil in a large frying pan over medium-high heat. Fry the chicken (and garlic, if using) for 5 minutes. Add the mushrooms and tomatoes and fry for a further 5 minutes.

Add the basil, wine and vinegar and stir through until boiling. Reduce the heat to low and cook for 20 minutes, adding some water if needed.

Cook the tagliatelle according to the packet directions and drain. Add to the sauce, season to taste and stir through for 1 minute.

Serve topped with basil leaves.

20 MIN

Pappardelle all'Arrabbiata

6 vine-ripened Roma tomatoes, coarsely chopped

½ cup (115g, 4oz) tomato paste

1 tbsp chilli flakes, or to taste

500g (1lb) pappardelle pasta

STAPLES

½ cup (125ml, 4fl oz) extra virgin olive oil

Salt

OPTIONAL

Basil or parsley leaves, to garnish

Parmesan cheese, grated, to garnish

Heat half the oil in a large frying pan over high heat. Add tomato, tomato paste and chilli to taste and cook, stirring occasionally, for 10 minutes or until thick and well flavoured.

Meanwhile, cook pasta according to the packet directions until al dente.

Drain pasta, reserving ¼ cup pasta water.

Add pasta to the pan with tomato mixture and stir to coat. Stir in remaining oil. Add a little reserved pasta water if needed to achieve a thick coating consistency.

Serve garnished with herbs and Parmesan.

1 HR

Classic Arancini

2 onions, finely chopped

3¼ cups (500g, 1lb) Arborio rice

1 cup (250ml, 8fl oz) dry white wine

8 cups (2L, 4pt) chicken stock

300g (10oz) buffalo mozzarella, cut into 1cm (½in) cubes

4 cups (500g, 16oz) breadcrumbs

STAPLES

30g (1oz) butter

1 tbsp olive oil

1 tsp salt

Plain flour, for dusting

Vegetable oil, for deep-frying

2-3 eggs, beaten

Heat butter and oil in a large saucepan over medium heat, add onion and saute for 10 minutes or until softened. Add rice, and stir to coat rice in oil. Add wine and stir for 3 minutes or until liquid is slightly reduced.

Add stock a ladleful at a time, stirring often and allowing some of the liquid to be absorbed before adding the next ladleful. Continue until all stock is added and rice is just cooked through (about 20 minutes). Stir in salt. Set aside to cool completely.

Take ¼ cup rice mixture, press a piece of mozzarella into the centre and mould with your hands to form a ball. Set aside on a baking tray lined with baking paper, and repeat with remaining rice and mozzarella.

Working with one arancini at a time, dust with flour, dip in beaten egg and roll in breadcrumbs to coat.

Heat 10cm (4in) oil in a deep-fryer or large saucepan to 180°C (350°F). Carefully add arancini in batches (the hot oil will spit). Cook for 8 minutes or until golden and crisp, turning occasionally. Remove with a slotted spoon and set aside in a warm place on paper towels. Repeat with remaining arancini.

Scatter with salt and serve warm.

40 MIN

Pumpkin and Pesto Pasta

5 cups (700g, 1½ lb) pumpkin, cut into 3cm (1in) pieces

1 clove garlic, minced

400g (14oz) dried fusilli pasta

½ cup (120g, 4oz) pesto, pre-made (see recipe on p87) or shop bought

STAPLES

3 tbsps olive oil

Salt and pepper

OPTIONAL

Shaved Parmesan, to garnish

Baby spinach leaves, to garnish

Preheat the oven to 220°C (430°C, Gas Mark 7).

Place the pumpkin pieces on a baking tray, mix through the oil and garlic, and season to taste with salt and pepper. Roast for 30 minutes or until lightly golden, stirring once.

While the pumpkin is roasting, cook the pasta according to packet instructions until al dente. Drain the pasta and place in a serving bowl. Mix through the pumpkin and pesto, and garnish with shaved Parmesand and baby spinach leaves to serve.

15 MIN

 4 CUPS

Home-made Pesto Sauce

6 cloves garlic, roughly chopped

2 cups (100g, 3½ oz) fresh basil leaves

⅓ cup (50g, 2oz) pine nuts

½ cup (50g, 2oz) fresh Romano cheese, grated

STAPLES

¾ cup (200ml, 7fl oz) olive oil

Freshly ground salt and pepper

Add the garlic, basil, pine nuts and Romano to a blender.

Slowly add half of the olive oil while blending until you have a thick pesto. Add more oil if needed.

Season to taste with salt and pepper.

**45 MIN
+ DRAINING**

Sicilian Caponata

3 eggplants, thickly sliced

1 large onion, finely chopped

3 tbsps tomato paste

1 x 400g (14oz) diced tomatoes

3 tbsps capers

2 tsps lemon zest

STAPLES

¼ cup (60ml, 2fl oz) olive oil

2 tbsps red wine vinegar

2 tbsps balsamic vinegar

¼ cup (55g, 2oz) caster sugar

4 tbsps salt

Pepper

OPTIONAL

1 large clove garlic, crushed

Place the eggplants in a colander, toss with the salt and let sit for 1 hour to drain. Wipe off the salt, cut into 1cm (½ in) cubes.

Heat 2 tablespoons olive oil in a large frying pan over medium heat and fry the onion (and garlic, if using) for 5 minutes. Add the rest of the oil and the eggplant and saute for 10 minutes.

Add the tomato paste and stir through for one minute. Add the tomatoes, vinegars and sugar and bring to a boil. Reduce heat to low and cook, covered, for 30 minutes. Add water as needed if it gets too dry.

Stir through the capers and zest, season to taste and serve.

25 MIN

Spinach and Mozzarella Piadina

4 cups (120g, 4oz) spinach leaves, rinsed

2 cloves garlic, crushed

115g (4oz) chilled lard, coarsely chopped

4 balls buffalo mozzarella, sliced

STAPLES

⅓ cup (80ml, 3fl oz) olive oil

3½ cups (435g, 14oz) plain flour

½ tsp bicarbonate of soda

1 tsp salt

1 cup (250ml, 8fl oz) cold water

Heat 1 tablespoon oil in a large frying pan over medium heat, add spinach and garlic and stir for 2 minutes or until wilted. Set aside.

Sift flour, bicarb and salt into a large bowl. Add lard and rub in with your fingertips until mixture resembles coarse crumbs. Add water and 1 tablespoon olive oil and stir to form a soft dough. Turn onto a lightly floured work surface and knead until smooth and elastic. Divide into eight equal pieces. Roll out each piece to 3mm (⅛ in) thick.

Heat 1 teaspoon olive oil in a frying pan over high heat. Add one piece of dough and cook for 2 minutes or until golden underneath. Flip and spread with about one-eighth each of the spinach mixture and the sliced mozzarella. Cook until piadina is light golden underneath and cheese is melting. Fold in half and press with a spatula. Transfer to a chopping board, cut into wedges and serve immediately.

Repeat with remaining olive oil, dough, spinach and mozzarella.

1 HR, 20 MIN

Italian-Style Stuffed Red Capsicums

4 large red
capsicums

200g (7oz) minced
pork

1 onion, finely
chopped

2 cloves garlic,
crushed

½ cup (80g, 3oz)
brown rice

2 cups (500ml, 1pt)
chicken stock

STAPLES

3 tbsps olive oil

OPTIONAL

Lemon wedges,
to garnish

2 tbsps parsley,
finely chopped,
to garnish

Preheat the oven to 200°C (400°F, Gas Mark 6).

Heat 2 tablespoons of oil in a saucepan over high heat. Add pork, onion and garlic and cook, stirring often, for 5 minutes or until pork is broken up and onion is softened. Add rice and stock, bring to the boil, reduce heat to low, cover and simmer for 25 minutes or until rice is almost tender and most stock is absorbed. Stir in parsley and set aside.

Cut stem end from capsicums and remove seeds. Rub outside of capsicums with remaining oil. Place on a baking tray lined with baking paper.

Fill capsicums with pork mixture. Transfer to the oven to roast for 45 minutes or until capsicums are slightly blackened and very tender.

Serve garnished with lemon wedges and parsley.

45 MIN

 4

Orzotto (Mushroom and Barley Risotto)

1 cup (200g, 7oz) pearl barley

4 cups (1L, 2pt) chicken or vegetable stock

350g (12oz) button mushrooms, sliced

1 clove garlic, minced

½ cup (50g, 2oz) Parmesan cheese, grated

STAPLES

2 tsps olive oil

1 tbsp unsalted butter

Salt and pepper

In a medium saucepan, boil the barley for 15 minutes with a pinch of salt. Drain then set aside. In a separate medium saucepan, bring the stock to a boil before reducing the heat to a very low setting to keep the stock warm.

Heat the olive oil in a large saucepan. Add the mushrooms and garlic and season with salt and pepper. Over a medium-high heat, cook while stirring until the mushrooms are soft and the garlic is fragrant. Add the barley and stir for 1 further minute or until the barley is coated.

Add 1 cup of stock and cook over a medium-low heat, stirring continuously, until nearly all the liquid is absorbed. Repeat the process with the stock until the barley is al dente and covered in sauce. Stir in butter.

Season with salt and pepper and garnish with Parmesan to serve.

25 MIN

Prawn Pizza

2 pre-made or
shop-bought pizza
bases

⅓ cup (70g, 2½ oz)
tomato paste

12 black olives,
pitted and sliced

2 cloves garlic,
minced

2½ cups (300g,
10oz) mozzarella
cheese, grated

300g (10oz)
prawn tails, shells
removed

STAPLES

2 tsps water

1 tbsp olive oil

Salt and pepper

Preheat oven to 180°C (350°F, Gas Mark 4).
Flour two baking trays, and place pizza bases
on them.

In a small bowl, mix together tomato paste,
water and garlic. Spread each base with the
mixture and scatter over the mozzarella.

Bake in the oven for 5 minutes or until
heated through, then remove from the
oven. Arrange olives and prawns over the
bases. Drizzle the olive oil over and season
with salt and pepper.

Bake in the oven for a further 10 minutes or
until the seafood is cooked. Remove from
the oven and serve.

Salami Pizza

2 pre-made or shop-bought pizza bases

¾ cup (175g, 6oz) tomato passata

½ tbsp mixed herbs

300g (10oz) mozzarella, thinly sliced

200g (7oz) hot salami, thinly sliced

12 cherry tomatoes, cut into quarters

STAPLES

¼ tsp sugar

OPTIONAL

2 tbsps green chilli, sliced

1 cup (30g, 1oz) rocket leaves

Preheat the oven to 180°C (350°F, Gas Mark 4). Lightly oil two pizza trays.

Place the passata, herbs and sugar in a small saucepan, with a couple of grinds of salt and pepper and bring to a boil. Reduce to low and simmer for 5 minutes until thickened.

Spread the sauce over the bases. Top with mozzarella, salami and tomatoes, and sliced chilli if desired.

Bake for 15 minutes or until the cheese is melted and slightly browned on the edges.

Top with the rocket, if using, to serve.

1 HR

4

Italian-Style Meatloaf

150g (5oz) pancetta, chopped

1 large onion, finely chopped

1kg (2lb) minced beef

1 cup (125g, 4oz) breadcrumbs

1 cup (125g, 4oz) Pecorino cheese, grated

1 cup (225g, 8oz) tomato passata

STAPLES

1 egg, beaten

1 tsp olive oil

1 tsp salt

1 tsp pepper

2 tbsps vinegar

2 tbsps brown sugar

Preheat oven to 190°C (375°F, Gas Mark 5) and oil a 23 x 12cm (9 x 5in) loaf tin.

Place the pancetta, onion, mince, breadcrumbs, cheese, egg, oil, salt and pepper in a bowl and mix together thoroughly. Press the mixture into the loaf tin.

Whisk together the tomato passata, vinegar and brown sugar. Add a couple of grinds of salt and pepper and spread ¼ cup of the mixture over the top of the meatloaf.

Bake the meatloaf for 50 minutes until browned and cooked through.

Spread the rest of the sauce over the top and serve hot.

50 MIN

Chicken Cacciatore

1 large onion, finely chopped

1.2kg (2½ lbs) chicken thigh fillets, cut into thirds

1 cup (250ml, 8fl oz) chicken stock

2 x 400g (14oz) cans diced tomatoes

2 cups (280g, 10oz) Kalamata olives, pitted

3 tbsps capers

STAPLES

2 tbsps olive oil

1 tsp sugar

Freshly ground salt and pepper

OPTIONAL

1 tbsp dried mixed herbs

Fresh basil leaves, shredded, to garnish

Heat half the oil in a large frying pan over medium heat and fry the onion for 5 minutes. Add the rest of the oil and fry the chicken pieces in batches for 4 minutes on each side until slightly browned

Return all the chicken to the pan and stir in the stock, tomatoes, sugar and dried herbs, if using. Bring to a boil, then reduce to a simmer. Cover and cook for 30 minutes.

Stir in the olives and capers and cook for another 5 minutes.

Season to taste and serve garnished with basil leaves.

30 MIN

Swordfish Ragu

500g (1lb) swordfish steaks, patted dry and cut into 1cm (½ in) cubes

1 large onion, finely chopped

300g (10oz) small button mushrooms, halved

½ cup (125ml, 4fl oz) white wine or vegetable stock

2 cups (450g, 1lb) diced tomatoes

¼ cup (35g, 1¼ oz) capers

STAPLES

3 tbsps olive oil

Freshly ground salt and pepper

OPTIONAL

Cooked spaghetti, to serve

Fresh parsley, chopped, to garnish

Lemon zest, to garnish

Heat half the oil in a large frying pan over medium heat and fry the onion for 5 minutes until softened.

Add the rest of the oil and fry the swordfish for 3 minutes, then add the mushrooms and saute for another 3 minutes.

Increase the heat to high and pour in the wine (or stock) and cook for 1 minute.

Add the tomatoes and bring to a boil, then immediately reduce to low heat and cook for 5 more minutes. Stir through the capers and season to taste.

Serve with spaghetti and garnish with parsley and lemon zest, if desired.

1 HR, 20 MIN

Spinach Lasagne

2 bunches of spinach, or 300g (10oz) frozen spinach

2 cups (450g, 1lb) cottage cheese (or ricotta)

2 cups (250g, 8oz) mozzarella cheese, grated

1 tsp dried oregano

2 cups (500g, 1lb) passata

9 lasagne sheets

STAPLES

1 egg

1 tsp salt

¼ tsp pepper

Preheat the oven to 180°C (350°F, Gas Mark 4).

If using fresh spinach, rinse, drain, pat dry and finely chop. If using frozen, ensure it is thawed before proceeding.

In a large bowl combine the spinach, cottage cheese (or ricotta), half of the mozzarella, oregano, egg, salt and pepper.

Lightly oil a large, deep-sided oven dish. Start by spreading a third of the passata in the dish. Then add lasagne, using as many sheets as needed to fill the dish in a single layer. Add spinach-cheese mixture next, and then repeat the layering, finishing with passata. Sprinkle the remaining mozzarella on top of this final layer.

Transfer to the oven to bake for 1 hour. Check after 45 minutes and if the top is browning too much cover with foil and return to the oven for the last 15 minutes.

Remove from the oven and set aside to cool slightly for 15 minutes before serving

45 MIN

Creamy Vegetarian Risotto

6 large spring onions, white part only, finely chopped

1 cup (155g, 5oz) celeriac, finely chopped

2¼ cups (350g, 12oz) Arborio rice

6 cups (1.5L, 50fl oz) hot vegetable stock

½ cup (50g, 2oz) Romano cheese, grated

1 cup (125g, 4oz) toasted hazelnuts, roughly chopped

STAPLES

2 tbsps unsalted butter

1 tbsp olive oil

OPTIONAL

2 cloves garlic, crushed

2 tbsps grated lemon rind

4 sprigs thyme, to garnish

Heat half the butter and the oil in a large, deep-sided frying pan over medium heat. Fry the spring onion and celeriac (and garlic if using) for 5 minutes. Don't let it brown.

Add the rice and stir for 1 minute. Increase the heat to medium-high and pour in 1 cup of stock and stir through the risotto until absorbed. Repeat with 1 cup of stock at a time until the risotto is tender.

Turn the heat to low, stir through the Romano and remaining butter.

Season to taste and serve topped with hazelnuts and thyme.

Caramelised Onion and Anchovy Tart

4 onions, sliced

2 tbsps fresh thyme, chopped

2 sheets puff pastry

½ cup (65g, 2oz) black olives, seeded and halved

1 small jar anchovies, drained and separated

STAPLES

3 tbsps olive oil

1 tsp brown sugar

1 tbsp balsamic vinegar

Preheat oven to 200°C (400°F, Gas Mark 6) and lightly oil a large baking tray. In a medium saucepan, heat the olive oil over medium heat. Add the sliced onions and gently cook for 15 minutes, stirring frequently, until softened.

Add the thyme, sugar and balsamic vinegar and stir for another 10 minutes until the onions are soft and sticky. Turn off the heat and let it sit.

Lay out the puff pastry to make a large rectangle with two ends overlapping slightly. Prick the sheets all over with a fork, and gently score a border around the edge 1½ cm (¾ in) thick.

Spread the onion mixture onto the pastry, keeping the border clear. Arrange the olives and the anchovies over the top. Bake in the oven for 20 minutes until the pastry is golden.

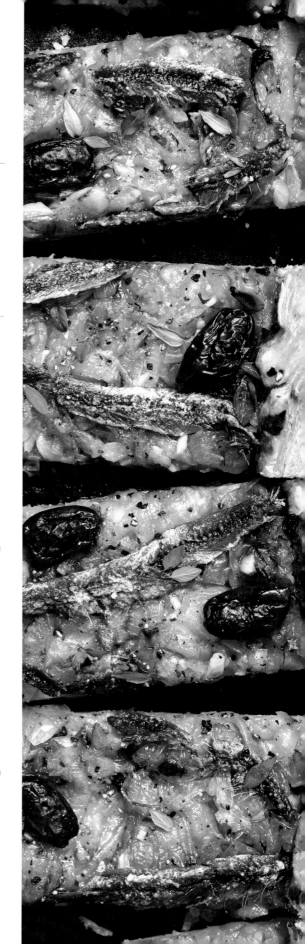

40 MIN

Chicken Parmigiana

4 x 200g (7oz) chicken breast fillets, pounded and flattened

1 cup (125g, 4oz) fresh breadcrumbs

1 small onion, finely chopped

1 clove garlic, crushed

3 cups (700g, 1½ lb) tomato passata

150g (5oz) mozzarella, cut into thick slices

STAPLES

¼ cup (30g, 1oz) plain flour

1 large egg, lightly beaten

Freshly ground salt and pepper

Olive oil, for frying

OPTIONAL

Cooked spaghetti, to serve

Fresh parsley, finely chopped, to garnish

Preheat oven to 190°C (375°F, Gas Mark 5).

Dredge the chicken in the flour, then the egg and then the breadcrumbs. Set aside.

Heat 1 ½ tablespoons of oil in a saucepan over medium heat and fry the onion and garlic for 5 minutes. Add the passata and bring to a boil. Reduce to a simmer for 15 minutes until thickened. Season to taste.

In a large deep-sided frying pan, heat 1cm (½ in) of oil over medium-high heat. Fry the chicken for 3 ½ minutes on each side then place on a large baking tray. Spoon ½ cup of sauce over them and place the mozzarella on top. Bake for 10 minutes.

Stir 1 cup of sauce through the spaghetti. Serve the Parmigianas over the spaghetti and garnish with parsley.

15 MIN

4

Tuna and Bean Salad

2 x 400g (14oz) cans cannellini beans, drained and rinsed

1 cup (250g, 9oz) cherry tomatoes, quartered

1 x 425g (15oz) can tuna, drained and flaked

1 large red onion, quartered and finely sliced

2 tbsps lemon juice

¼ cup (10g, ¼ oz) fresh parsley, finely chopped

STAPLES

1½ tbsps apple cider vinegar

1½ tbsps olive oil

Freshly ground salt and pepper

Place the beans, tomatoes, tuna, onion and parsley in a large salad bowl.

Whisk together the lemon juice, vinegar, oil and a few grinds of salt and pepper.

Pour the dressing over the salad and gently toss to combine.

Season further to taste and serve.

**25 MIN
+ SETTING**

 8

Tiramisu

2½ cups (550ml, 20fl oz) espresso or very strong black coffee, cooled

2 cups (460g, 1lb) mascarpone cheese

400g (14oz) lady finger biscuits – crisp, not sponge

150g (5oz) plain dark chocolate, grated

2½ tsps unsweetened cocoa powder

STAPLES

2 large eggs

⅓ cup (70g, 2½ oz) caster sugar

Separate the eggs. In a medium bowl, whisk the egg yolks and sugar together until the mixture is thick, pale yellow, and forms a ribbon when the whisk is lifted out of the bowl (about 1 minute). Add ¼ cup of coffee and the mascarpone and whisk until the mixture is smooth.

In a separate bowl, whisk the egg whites until soft peaks form when you lift the whisk out of the bowl. Gently fold the egg white into the mascarpone mixture.

Dip the biscuits, one at a time, into the remaining coffee; let them soak just long enough to become damp but not soggy.

Place one or two biscuits into the bottom of each glass or serving bowl – enough to form a layer. Break the biscuits up if you need to. Sprinkle over about ½ teaspoon of the grated chocolate and layer over that around 2cm (1in) of the mascarpone mixture. Repeat biscuit, chocolate and mascarpone layers until you get to the top of the glass or bowl then cover with plastic wrap and leave in the fridge until the mascarpone mixture is set, 8-10 hours or overnight.

When you are ready to serve, place the cocoa powder in a small sieve and dust over the top of the tiramisu.

30 MIN
+ CHILLING + FREEZING

Cherry Gelato

1¾ cup (350g, 12oz) cherries, pitted (fresh or from a jar)

1 cup (250ml, 8fl oz) single cream

6 large egg yolks

1 cup (250ml, 8fl oz) thickened cream

STAPLES

1 cup (250ml, 8fl oz) milk

1 tsp vanilla extract

¾ cup (165g, 6oz) caster sugar

Reserve a handful of cherries for garnish and puree the rest in a blender until smooth. Set aside.

Bring the milk and cream to a boil in a large heavy saucepan.

Stir in the vanilla extract and remove from the heat and let it cool.

In another bowl, whisk together the sugar and egg yolks.

Gently reheat the milk mixture until almost simmering, then pour in a thin stream into the egg-yolk mix and whisk it in as you pour.

Add the mixture back to the saucepan and gently heat over low-medium heat for 5 minutes or until it begins to thicken. Do not let it boil.

Remove from the heat and stir in the thickened cream. Then stir through the cherry puree (it doesn't have be thoroughly mixed, if you roughly mix it through, you'll have an attractive streaked pattern through the gelato).

Refrigerate until cold, stirring every 30 minutes for 2 hours.

Transfer to a freezer container, then freeze for at least 5 hours, preferably overnight.

Serve decorated with reserved cherries on top.

lebanese

10 MIN

2

CUPS

Hummus

2 x 400g (14oz)
cans chickpeas,
drained and rinsed

2 small cloves
garlic, crushed

½ cup (115g, 4oz)
tahini paste

3 tsps ground
cumin

¼ cup (50ml, 2fl oz)
lemon juice

STAPLES

3 tbsps olive oil

2 tsps salt

OPTIONAL

1 tsp paprika,
to garnish

Place the tahini and olive oil in a food
processor or blender and blend until
smooth.

Add half the chickpeas and puree
until smooth.

Add the rest of the ingredients and puree.
Add water if it's too thick.

Season further to taste and serve
sprinkled with paprika.

1 HR, 10 MIN

Tabbouleh

1 cup (180g, 6oz) bulgur

4 cups (185g, 6oz) fresh parsley, chopped

1 cup (45g, 1½ oz) fresh mint, finely chopped

5 spring onions, finely chopped

⅓ cup (70ml, 2½ fl oz) lemon juice

5 Roma tomatoes, seeded and chopped

STAPLES

⅓ cup (70ml, 2½ fl oz) olive oil

Freshly ground salt and pepper

Place the bulgur in a large heatproof bowl and cover with boiling water. Leave to soak for 30 minutes. Drain, then place the bulgur in a clean tea towel and use it to squeeze out any excess water.

Place the bulgur in a large salad bowl with the parsley, mint and spring onions.

Whisk together the lemon juice, oil and a couple of good grinds of salt and pepper.

Pour over the salad and toss to combine. Let sit for 30 minutes to let the flavours infuse into the bulgur.

Toss through the tomatoes just before serving and season further to taste.

1 HR, 15 MIN

Beetroot Falafel

2 beetroots, peeled and cut into 1cm (½ in) cubes

3 cloves garlic, chopped

2 cups (320g, 11oz) tinned chickpeas, drained and rinsed

1½ tbsps ground cumin

1½ tbsps ground coriander

1 cup (250ml, 8fl oz) tahini sauce, to serve (shop-bought or see recipe page 118)

STAPLES

1 tsp salt

1 tbsp olive oil

OPTIONAL

1 tbsp grated ginger

4 cups (120g, 4oz) mixed salad leaves

Lemon wedges, to serve

Steam the beetroot for 15 minutes until tender and let cool for 30 minutes.

Preheat the oven to 190°C (375°F, Gas Mark 5) and line a large flat baking tray with baking paper.

Place the garlic (and ginger, if using) in a food processor or blender and blitz until combined.

Add the beetroot, chickpeas, cumin, coriander and salt. Pulse until the mixture is well combined but still slightly chunky.

Form into small balls and place on the baking paper. Drizzle over some olive oil and bake for 20 minutes until cooked through.

Serve the falafel with tahini sauce and salad leaves and lemon wedges on the side.

25 MIN
+ SOAKING + CHILLING

Classic Chickpea Falafel

2 cups (350g, 12oz) dried chickpeas, soaked in cold water overnight, drained and rinsed

1 onion, roughly chopped

¼ cup (10g, ¼ oz) parsley, coarsely chopped

2 tsps ground cumin

1 tsp ground coriander

¼ tsp cayenne pepper

STAPLES

2 tbsps plain flour

1 egg

¼ tsp pepper

2 tsps salt

Oil, for deep-frying

Place the chickpeas in the bowl of a large food processor and process until finely ground. Add the onion, parsley, flour, egg, spices, pepper and salt and pulse until smooth.

Transfer to a container, cover and refrigerate for at least 1 hour or overnight.

Form mixture into rounds about the size of a golf ball and flatten slightly.

Heat 10cm (4in) oil in a deep-fryer or large saucepan to 180°C (350°F). Carefully add 4–6 falafel. Cook for 5 minutes until golden, turning occasionally.

Remove with a slotted spoon and set aside in a warm place on paper towels. Repeat with remaining falafel.

10 MIN

2

CUPS

Tahini Sauce

4 cups (640g, 1lb 6oz) sesame seeds

1 tbsp lemon juice

STAPLES

2 tbsps olive oil

1 tsp salt

Heat a large frying pan over medium heat. Dry fry the sesame seeds ¼ cup at a time, constantly tossing. As soon as they begin to brown, immediately remove each batch to a blender or food processor bowl.

Add the lemon juice, half the oil and salt to the blender and puree until smooth. Add more oil as needed until creamy.

Season to taste before serving.

Will keep for up to 2 weeks in a sealed container in the refrigerator.

1 HR, 15 MIN

Spicy Sweet Potato Falafel

2 cups (300g, 10oz) sweet potato, peeled and cut into 1cm (½ in) cubes

3 cloves garlic, crushed

2 cups (320g, 11oz) tinned chickpeas, drained and rinsed

1½ tbsps ground cumin

1½ tbsps ground oregano

1 tsp turmeric

STAPLES

1 tsp salt

Freshly ground pepper

OPTIONAL

1 cup (250ml, 8fl oz) tahini sauce, to serve (shop-bought or see recipe page 118)

Lemon wedges, to serve

Steam the sweet potato for 15 minutes until tender and let cool for 30 minutes.

Preheat the oven to 190°C (375°F, Gas Mark 5) and line a large flat baking tray with baking paper.

Place the sweet potato, garlic, chickpeas, turmeric, cumin, oregano, salt and a couple of grinds of pepper in a blender or food processor. Pulse until the mixture is well combined but still slightly chunky.

Form into small balls and place on the baking paper. Drizzle over some olive oil and bake for 20 minutes until cooked through.

Serve the falafel with tahini sauce and salad leaves and lemon wedges on the side.

20 MIN

Couscous and Zucchini Salad

1 cup (170g, 6oz) pearl couscous

2 medium zucchinis, ends trimmed, halved lengthways and sliced

4 large spring onions, green parts finely chopped

2 small cloves garlic, crushed

1 lemon, zested and juiced

STAPLES

1½ cups (360ml, 12fl oz) water

1½ tbsps butter

1 tbsp olive oil

Freshly ground salt and pepper

OPTIONAL

1 cup (15g, ½ oz) fresh basil leaves, to garnish

Bring the water to a boil in a large saucepan and add the couscous. Reduce heat to low, cover and simmer for 8 minutes or until the couscous is cooked. Add more water as needed and stir frequently.

In a large frying pan, melt the butter and olive oil over medium heat and fry the zucchini, spring onions and garlic for 5 minutes until the zucchini is tender.

Add the couscous, zest and half the juice. Season to taste and add more juice if needed.

Serve garnished with basil leaves.

15 MIN + DRAINING

2 CUPS

Labneh Za'atar Dip

2 cups (500ml, 1pt) Greek yoghurt (full fat)

2 tbsps za'atar (shop-bought or see recipe page 148)

1 small spring onion, finely chopped

2 tbsps fresh mint, finely chopped

4 portions Lebanese flatbread

STAPLES

½ cup (125ml, 4fl oz) olive oil

Place a large, clean cheesecloth in a double layer in a colander in a large bowl. Pour the yoghurt onto the middle of the cloth. Bring up the sides of the cloth and twist tightly to squeeze excess liquid from the yoghurt. Tie the cloth tightly and place everything in the refrigerator for 2 days to drain.

The labneh should be as thick as whipped cream.

Whisk through 1 teaspoon olive oil and top with za'atar, parsley and spring onions and drizzle some more oil over the top.

Brush the flatbread with the rest of the oil and heat for 1 minute on each side in a hot frying pan. Cut into small pieces and serve with the labneh dip.

Sumac Roast Chicken

2 medium roasting chickens (size 16)

2 tbsps sumac

2 tsps smoked paprika

½ tsp cayenne pepper

4 small lemons; 2 whole, 1 cut into wedges, 1 zested

3 large cloves garlic, crushed

STAPLES

2 tsps brown sugar

3 tbsps olive oil

2 tbsps salt

Freshly ground pepper

OPTIONAL

6 sprigs thyme, to garnish

Preheat oven to 220°C (425°F, Gas Mark 7). Pat dry the chickens and place in a large roasting tin big enough to fit both comfortably.

Place the sumac, paprika, cayenne, lemon zest, garlic, sugar, oil, salt and a couple of grinds of pepper in a bowl and mix thoroughly.

Coat the chickens in the sumac mixture and push a whole lemon into the cavity of each chicken.

Place the chickens in the oven and bake for 20 minutes. Reduce the heat to 190°C (375°F, Gas Mark 5) and roast for another 50 minutes or until the chickens are browned and cooked through.

Serve the chicken garnished with thyme leaves and with lemon wedges on the side.

4

Spiced Chicken with Pomegranate Couscous

800g (1¾ lb) chicken breast fillets, cut into large pieces

1 tsp ground cumin

1 tsp ground oregano

½ tsp sumac

Seeds from 1 pomegranate

2 cups (380g, 14oz) couscous

STAPLES

2¼ cups (560ml, 19 fl oz) water

2 tbsps butter

2 tbsps olive oil

1 tsp salt

Freshly ground pepper

OPTIONAL

¼ cup (5g, ¼ oz) mint leaves, to garnish

250g (9oz) feta, crumbled

Place the couscous in a heatproof bowl. Bring the water and butter to the boil. Pour over the couscous, cover the bowl with a tight-fitting lid and let it sit for 5 minutes until all the liquid is absorbed. Fluff the couscous up with a fork and set aside.

Mix together the cumin, oregano, sumac, half the oil, the salt and a couple of grinds of pepper.

Place the chicken in a large bowl, add the spice mix and toss to coat the chicken.

Heat the rest of the oil in a large frying pan and fry the chicken in batches for 5 minutes on each side until cooked through.

Mix the mint leaves and pomegranate seeds through the couscous and serve the warm chicken on top of portions of couscous. Serve with crumbled feta if desired.

20 MIN + MARINATING

Spiced Chicken Skewers

800g (1¾ lb) chicken breast fillets, cut into 1½ cm (¾ in) cubes

¼ cup (15g, ½ oz) semi-dried tomatoes, finely chopped

1 tbsp ground oregano

1 tbsp ground cumin

½ tsp sumac

½ cup (20g, ¾ oz) fresh parsley, roughly chopped

12 wooden skewers, soaked in hot water for 30 minutes

STAPLES

2 tbsps olive oil

Freshly ground salt and pepper

Mix together the oil, semi-dried tomatoes, oregano, cumin, sumac and a couple of grinds of salt and pepper.

Place the chicken in a bowl and coat with the spice mix. Let marinate in the refrigerator for at least 1 hour.

Heat a grill pan over medium-high heat.

Thread the chicken pieces onto the skewers. Grill the skewers for 10 minutes, turning every 2 minutes or so.

Serve the skewers hot garnished with parsley.

15 MIN

Lebanese-Style Pomegranate Salad

4 cups (500g, 1lb 2oz) tightly packed silverbeet, stems removed, roughly chopped

2 x 400g (14oz) cans chickpeas, drained and rinsed

Seeds from 2 pomegranates

¼ cup (60ml, 2fl oz) lemon juice

1 tsp sumac

2 tsps ground cumin

STAPLES

¼ cup (60ml, 2fl oz) olive oil

Freshly ground salt and pepper

Place the silverbeet, chickpeas and pomegranate seeds in a large salad bowl.

Whisk together the lemon juice, sumac, cumin, olive oil and a couple of grinds of salt and pepper.

Pour over the salad and toss to combine. Season to taste and serve.

Butternut Pumpkin with Chickpeas and Tahini

2 small butternut pumpkins, halved lengthways and seeds removed

1 x 400g (14oz) can chickpeas, drained and rinsed

3 cloves garlic, minced

2 tsps ground cumin

2 tbsps dried oregano

⅔ cup (160ml, 5fl oz) tahini sauce (shop-bought or see recipe page 118)

STAPLES

⅓ cup (75ml, 2½ fl oz) olive oil

Freshly ground salt and pepper

OPTIONAL

1 tsp ground coriander

Sprigs of coriander, to garnish

Preheat the oven to 180°C (350°F, Gas Mark 4).

Place the pumpkin halves skin side down on a baking tray and drizzle half the oil over the top and sprinkle over some salt and pepper. Roast them for 30 minutes until slightly softened.

Remove from the oven and let cool for 10 minutes. Scoop out the flesh and retain it, leaving at least 1cm (½ in) of flesh attached to the skin.

In a frying pan, heat the rest of the oil over medium heat and fry the garlic, cumin, half the oregano and the ground coriander, if using, for 1 minute. Add the chickpeas and half the scooped-out flesh. Fry for 8 minutes.

Stuff the pumpkin halves with equal portions of chickpea mixture then return to the oven and bake for 40 minutes until the pumpkins are completely cooked through and slightly crisp on the outside.

Serve the pumpkin halves drizzled with tahini sauce and garnished with the remaining oregano and fresh coriander leaves.

25 MIN

Crispy Fattoush

4 small Lebanese
cucumbers,
chopped

2 large tomatoes,
chopped

1 medium cos
lettuce, chopped

2 tbsps lemon juice

2 large pita breads

1½ tsps sumac

STAPLES

⅓ cup (80ml, 3fl oz)
olive oil

1½ tsps balsamic
vinegar

Freshly ground salt
and pepper

OPTIONAL

1 medium red
onion, chopped

1 green capsicum,
cut into small cubes

Brush the pita breads with 1½ tablespoons of the oil. Heat a large frying pan over medium heat and fry the pita breads for about 1½ minutes each side until they're just crispy and browned. Let them cool, then break them up into small pieces and set aside.

Place the cucumber, tomatoes and lettuce, plus onion and capsicum, if using, in a large salad bowl.

Whisk together the lemon juice, sumac, remaining oil and vinegar. Sprinkle over the salad and toss to combine.

Add the bread to the salad and toss again. Season to taste with salt and pepper and serve

NOTE: Fattoush is a Middle Eastern speciality salad. The crispy bread and sumac spice are essential to the dish, but it is perfectly okay to substitute preferred or available salad ingredients if you like.

20 MIN

Easy Manakish

2 tbsps sumac

3 tbsps dried oregano

3 tbsps dried thyme

¼ cup (40g, 1½ oz) sesame seeds

6 Lebanese flatbreads

STAPLES

½ cup (140ml, 5fl oz) olive oil

1 tsp salt

Preheat oven to 200°C (400°F, Gas Mark 6) and line two large flat baking trays with baking paper.

Heat a frying pan over medium heat and dry fry the sesame seeds for about 2 minutes until they just start to brown. Immediately remove the seeds from the pan into a small bowl.

Add the sumac, oregano, thyme, oil and salt. Mix together thoroughly then set aside.

Spread the mix over the flatbreads leaving a 1cm (½ in) edge. Place them on the baking trays and bake for 10 minutes until they start to brown slightly.

Serve hot.

Baba Ganoush

3 medium eggplants, halved and patted dry

1½ tbsps Greek yoghurt

4 cloves garlic, unpeeled

1 tbsp tahini paste

¼ cup (60ml, 2fl oz) lemon juice

½ tsp sumac

STAPLES

⅓ cup (80ml, 3fl oz) olive oil

Freshly ground salt and pepper

OPTIONAL

¼ tsp cayenne pepper

2 tbsps parsley, chopped

Preheat the oven to 230°C (450°F, Gas Mark 8). Line a large flat baking tray with baking paper.

Brush the eggplant halves with 1 teaspoon each of the olive oil and lightly coat the garlic cloves in oil. Place the eggplant on the tray and roast for 30 minutes, turning every 7 minutes until soft. Add the garlic for the last 15 minutes.

Place the eggplants and garlic in a sealable container and set aside for 30 minutes.

Scoop the flesh out of the eggplants and decant the garlic cloves. Place in a food processor or blender, add the tahini, lemon juice, remaining oil and a couple of grinds of salt and pepper. Blend until smooth and season to taste. Serve with the sumac, cayenne and parsley sprinkled over the top.

**25 MIN
+ CHILLING**

Vegan Falafel Wraps

1 x 400g (14oz) can chickpeas, drained and rinsed

1 onion, finely chopped

2 cloves garlic, crushed

1 tsp ground coriander

1 tsp ground cumin

4 wraps

STAPLES

2 tbsps plain flour

2 tsps salt

Vegetable oil, for frying

OPTIONAL

Tahini sauce, to serve (shop-bought or see recipe page 118)

Salad ingredients, to serve

Place the chickpeas, onion, garlic, coriander, cumin, flour and salt in a food processor. Blend until you have a smooth mixture. Place the mix in the refrigerator to chill for at least 30 minutes.

Shape the mixture into large bite-size balls, then flatten them slightly and place on a plate.

Fill a deep-sided frying pan with 2cm (1in) oil and heat to 180°C (350°F), measured with a cooking thermometer. Fry the falafels for just over 2 minutes each side or until browned. Drain on paper towels.

Serve the falafel balls hot on wraps drizzled with tahini sauce and with preferred salad ingredients such as spinach leaves, tomato, alfalfa sprouts and parsley.

40 MIN

Salmon Tabbouleh Salad

1 cup (170g, 6oz) white quinoa

16 plum cherry tomatoes, halved

1 Continental cucumber, quartered lengthways and sliced

3 x 200g (7oz) salmon fillets, skin removed (or 600g/1lb 5oz canned salmon)

1½ cups (65g, 2oz) fresh parsley, chopped

2 large lemons; 1 juiced, 1 cut into wedges

STAPLES

2 cups (500ml, 1pt) water

⅓ cup (80ml, 3fl oz) olive oil

Freshly ground salt and pepper

2 cups (500ml, 1pt) water

Rinse the quinoa, then place in a pot with the water, lightly salted. Bring to a boil, then reduce to a simmer for 15 minutes or until the quinoa is tender. Set aside to let it cool.

Brush the salmon lightly with oil and heat a frying pan over medium-high heat. Drizzle a little lemon juice over the fillets and then grill 3 minutes each side or until completely cooked through. Break up the fillets into flakes and set aside to cool for 20 minutes.

Place the quinoa, tomatoes, cucumber, parsley and cooked or tinned salmon together in a large salad bowl. Whisk together the remaining lemon juice and oil with a couple of grinds of salt and pepper. Drizzle over the salad then toss to combine.

Season further to taste and serve with lemon wedges on the side.

2 HR

Persian Lamb and Eggplant Ragu

12 Lebanese
eggplants, ends
trimmed

1kg (2lb) lamb
chops, cut into 2cm
(1in) chunks, bones
removed

2 medium onions
chopped

1 x 400g (14oz) can
diced tomatoes

⅔ cup (160ml, 5fl
oz) Greek yoghurt

1½ tsps turmeric

STAPLES

⅓ cup (100ml,
3½ fl oz) olive oil

OPTIONAL

½ tsp cinnamon

¼ cup (60ml, 2fl oz)
lemon juice

Heat half the oil in a flameproof casserole
dish over medium heat. Fry the onion for
5 minutes until softened. Increase heat to
medium-high and fry the lamb in batches
until browned.

Return the lamb to the pan and add the
spices, lemon juice, if using, and enough
water to cover the lamb. Reduce heat to
low, cover and simmer for 50 minutes.

Heat the rest of the oil in another pan
over medium heat and fry the eggplants for
6 minutes, turning frequently. Add to the
stew for a further 40 minutes.

Ten minutes before the stew is ready,
scoop out ¼ cup of the liquid and mix
through the yoghurt then stir the yoghurt
through the stew. Season to taste and serve.

1 HR

 4

Easy Pilaf

1 large onion, chopped

1 cup (125g, 4oz) almonds

½ cup (60g, 2oz) chopped walnuts

2 x 400g (14oz) cans chickpeas, drained and rinsed

1 cup (155g, 4oz) long-grain rice (basmati or jasmine)

1 tsp ground coriander

STAPLES

2 tbsps olive oil

Freshly ground salt and pepper

3 cups (750ml, 24fl oz) water (or use vegetable stock)

OPTIONAL

½ cup (75g, 3oz) prunes, pitted and chopped

1 tsp ground cumin

¼ tsp ground cardamom

Heat the oil in a large heatproof casserole dish over medium heat and fry the onion for 5 minutes. Increase the heat to high and add the almonds and walnuts and fry for 2 minutes to toast the nuts.

Stir in the coriander, and cumin and cardamom, if using, for 1 minute, then add the rice and stir for 1 minute. Pour in the water (or stock) and chickpeas and bring to a boil.

Reduce heat to low, cover and cook for 40 minutes. Stir through the prunes, if using, then cook for a further 10 minutes, covered.

Season to taste and serve.

40 MIN

Lebanese Meat Pies (Fatayer)

4 sheets shortcrust pastry

500g (1lb) minced lamb

1 small onion, finely chopped

1 tomato, seeded and finely chopped

½ cup (70g, 2½ oz) pine nuts, half ground in a mortar and pestle to a paste

1 tsp sumac

STAPLES

½ tbsp olive oil

Freshly ground salt and pepper

OPTIONAL

1 tsp za'atar spice mix (shop-bought or see recipe page 148)

Preheat the oven to 200°C (400°F, Gas Mark 6) and line a large baking tray with baking paper.

Place the lamb, onion, tomato, pine nut paste, sumac (and za'atar, if using) and a couple of grinds of salt and pepper in a large bowl and mix together thoroughly.

Cut the pastry sheets in half. Shape the mix into 8 thick tapered sausages and place along the middle of each pastry sheet. Fold up the sides of the pastry and pinch the ends of the pastry together to form a little 'boat' around the lamb.

Sprinkle a few of the remaining pine nuts over each pie and bake for at least 15 minutes until the pastry is browned and the lamb mix is cooked through.

20 MIN

Hummus Fatteh

3 large pita breads, torn into pieces

2 x 400g (14oz) cans chickpeas, drained and rinsed

1½ cups (375ml, 13fl oz) Greek yoghurt

4 small cloves garlic, crushed

¼ cup (60ml, 2fl oz) lemon juice

3 tbsps tahini paste

STAPLES

2 tbsp olive oil

Freshly ground salt and pepper

OPTIONAL

⅓ cup (45g, 1½ oz) toasted pine nuts, to garnish

1 tbsp sumac, to garnish

Fresh parsley, roughly chopped, to garnish

Toss the bread and half the oil together in a bowl, then toast the bread in a pan on medium heat until browned and crisp. Set aside.

Place the yoghurt, ⅔ cup chickpeas, garlic, half the lemon juice, tahini and a couple of grinds of salt and pepper in a food processor and puree until smooth. Add more lemon juice to taste.

Arrange the bread on a large serving plate, spoon over the yoghurt mix and top with extra chickpeas.

If desired, top with the pine nuts and parsley and dust with the sumac to serve.

50 MIN

Chickpea Stew

2 x 400g (14oz)
cans chickpeas,
drained and rinsed

1 large onion,
chopped

1 x 400g (14oz) can
diced tomatoes

1 tbsp za'atar
(shop-bought or
see recipe page
148)

3 tbsps tomato
paste

400g (14oz) green
beans, cut into 4cm
(1½ in) lengths

STAPLES

2 tbsps olive oil

1¼ cups (300ml,
10fl oz) water

Freshly ground salt
and pepper

OPTIONAL

4 large cloves
garlic, crushed

Heat the oil in a large heatproof casserole dish over medium heat. Fry the onion for 3 minutes then add the garlic, if using, and fry for 2 more minutes. Stir in the za'atar and tomato paste for 1 minute.

Add the tomatoes and chickpeas and water. Bring to a boil, then reduce heat to low, cover and simmer for 10 minutes. Stir through the beans and cook for another 20 minutes.

Season to taste and serve.

45 MIN

Stewed Green Beans

1 onion, quartered and finely sliced

3 cloves garlic, crushed

500g (1lb) green beans

1½ tsps cumin

1 cup (225g, 8oz) tomato passata

1 x 400g (14oz) can diced tomatoes

STAPLES

3 tbsps olive oil

Freshly ground salt and pepper

OPTIONAL

1 tsp cinnamon

Fresh parsley, chopped, to garnish

Heat the olive oil in a large saucepan over medium heat. Fry the onion and garlic for 5 minutes until the onion is softened. Add the cumin (and cinnamon, if using) and tomatoes and 1 teaspoon of salt and cook for a further 5 minutes.

Add the passata and beans, bring to a boil, then cover and turn the heat down to low. Simmer for 30 minutes until the beans are softened, adding any water as needed.

Season further to taste and serve hot or cold, garnished with parsley.

1 HR

Stuffed Zucchini

12 small Lebanese zucchinis

⅓ cup (60g, 2oz) long-grain rice (basmati or jasmine)

1 x 400g (14oz) can diced tomatoes, drained, juice reserved

1 small onion, finely chopped

¼ cup (30g, 1oz) slivered almonds, chopped

¼ cup (60ml, 2fl oz) lemon juice

STAPLES

⅓ cup (75ml, 2½ fl oz) olive oil

Freshly ground salt and pepper

2 cups (500ml, 1pt) water (or use vegetable stock)

OPTIONAL

2 tsps sweet paprika

Trim the stems from the zucchinis and carefully scoop out the flesh leaving about 5mm worth still attached to the skin. Keep the flesh.

Mix together the rice, tomato, onion, almonds, lemon juice and paprika, if using, and a couple of grinds of salt and pepper. Stuff each zucchini, leaving a 1½ cm (¾ in) gap from the end to let the mixture expand.

Arrange the zucchinis in a large heavy-based saucepan. Pour over the water (or stock). Cover and cook on low heat for at least 35 minutes until the rice is cooked and tender.

Serve hot or cold with the liquid from the pot.

Fish Pilaf

4 cups (650g, 1lb 7oz) cooked long-grain rice

400g (14oz) white fish fillets (snapper or flathead) cut into bite-size chunks

1 large onion, finely chopped

¾ cup (90g, 3oz) peanuts, roughly chopped

2 tsps ground cumin

2 tsps ground oregano

STAPLES

⅓ cup (100ml, 3½ fl oz) olive oil

Freshly ground salt and pepper

OPTIONAL

3 cloves garlic, crushed

Fresh parsley, chopped, to garnish

Red chillies, thinly sliced, to garnish

Heat half the oil in a large frying pan over medium heat and fry the onion, and garlic if using, for 5 minutes. Add the fish pieces and peanuts and fry everything for a further 5 minutes.

Stir in the cumin and oregano for 1 minute. Add the rice, the rest of the oil and salt and pepper to taste.

Heat through for 15 minutes over low heat until the rice is hot and the fish is cooked through.

Serve garnished with parsley, if desired.

50 MIN

Crispy Za'atar Fries

800g (1¾ lb) small new potatoes, cleaned and cut into wedges

2½ tbsps sesame seeds

½ tbsp sumac

1½ tbsps dried thyme

1½ tbsps dried oregano

2 tsps ground cumin

STAPLES

¼ cup (60ml, 2fl oz) olive oil

2 tbsps salt

Preheat oven to 200°C (400°F, Gas Mark 6) and line two large flat baking trays with baking paper. Fry the sesame seeds in a large frying pan over medium heat for 2 minutes. As soon as they begin to brown, remove them from the pan.

To make the za'atar, mix together 1 ½ tablespoons of the toasted sesame seeds with the sumac, thyme, oregano, cumin and salt.

Place the potatoes in a large bowl and drizzle the olive oil over the top. Sprinkle the za'atar over the potatoes as well and toss to coat.

Place the wedges in a single layer on the trays and bake for 40 minutes until soft and browned on the outside, turning halfway through.

Serve the fries hot sprinkled with the rest of the sesame seeds.

50 MIN

 4

Za'atar Chicken

1 batch za'atar
spice mix (shop-
bought or see
recipe page 148)

8 mixed chicken
pieces

STAPLES

⅓ cup (80ml, 3fl oz)
olive oil

OPTIONAL

Fattoush (see
recipe page 130),
or other salad, to
serve

Fresh parsley,
roughly chopped,
to garnish

Preheat the oven to 190°C (375°F, Gas
Mark 5).

Drizzle half the oil over the chicken pieces
and toss to coat. Sprinkle the za'atar mix
over the top and again toss to coat.

Place the pieces snugly in a casserole
dish, drizzle over the rest of the oil and
bake for 40 minutes until the chicken is
cooked through.

Serve with fattoush or other salad as desired,
garnished with parsley.

2 HR

Eggplant Salad

3 large eggplants

4 small cloves garlic, crushed

6 spring onions, chopped (reserve half of the green parts for garnish)

1½ tbsps lemon juice

1 tsp ground oregano

1 tsp ground cumin

STAPLES

2 tbsps olive oil

Freshly ground salt and pepper

Preheat the oven to 200°C (400°F, Gas Mark 6).

Pierce the eggplants all over with a fork. Rub them with half the olive oil, then roast whole on a baking tray for 55 minutes or until they have softened and have darkened in colour.

Let them sit for at least 30 minutes to cool.

Halve the eggplants and scoop out the flesh into a fine mesh sieve. Gently push the eggplant flesh down to remove some of the liquid.

In a small pan, heat the rest of the oil and fry the garlic, spring onion, oregano and cumin over medium heat for 4 minutes. Increase the heat to medium-high and add the eggplant flesh. Stir in the lemon juice and cook for 10 minutes.

Season to taste and serve garnished with the reserved spring onions.

50 MIN

Harissa-Roasted Eggplant with Lentil Salad

3 cups (600g, 1lb 5oz) cooked brown lentils

2 large eggplants, halved lengthways

1 cup (250ml, 8fl oz) Greek yoghurt

1 cup (15g, ½ oz) fresh dill, torn

1 cup (15g, ½ oz) fresh parsley leaves

⅓ cup (50g, 2oz) harissa spice mix

STAPLES

⅓ cup (70ml, 2½ fl oz) olive oil

Freshly ground salt and pepper

OPTIONAL

2 medium lemons, cut into wedges

Preheat the oven to 180°C (350°F, Gas Mark 4) and line a baking tray with baking paper.

Score the flesh of the eggplants with deep diagonal cuts to form diamond patterns.

Rub 1 tablespoon of the harissa mix into the cuts of each eggplant. Place cut side up on the baking tray and drizzle ½ tablespoon of olive oil over the top of each half.

Bake the eggplants for at least 30 minutes until the flesh is soft and cooked through.

Toss the lentils with the rest of the oil, the dill, parsley, three wedges' worth of lemon juice (if using) and a couple of grinds of salt and pepper.

Serve the eggplants with ¼ cup of yoghurt drizzled over the top and with the lentil salad and wedges on the side. Sprinkle the remaining harissa over the top.

30 MIN

Moroccan Cauliflower Steaks

1 large head cauliflower, cut into 1½ cm (¾ in) thick steaks

¾ cup (175g, 6oz) tomato passata

3 cloves garlic, crushed

1 tsp sweet paprika

1 tsp ground cumin

1 tbsp lemon juice

STAPLES

⅓ cup (80ml, 3fl oz) olive oil

Freshly ground salt and pepper

OPTIONAL

Fried potato wedges, to serve

Preheat the oven to 220°C (425°F, Gas Mark 7) and line two large flat baking trays with baking paper.

Mix together the passata, garlic, paprika, cumin, lemon juice and half the olive oil along with a couple of grinds of salt and pepper.

Place the steaks on the baking trays and brush the tops with the tomato mixture. Roast for 5 minutes, then turn and brush the other sides with the tomato mix and roast for another 5 minutes.

Heat a large frying pan over medium-high heat and fry the steaks for 2 minutes on each side, brushing over any leftover mixture.

Serve the steaks hot with potato wedges on the side.

4

Middle Eastern Spiced Meatballs

600g (1lb 5oz) minced lamb

1 small onion, grated and squeezed to remove excess liquid

2 cloves garlic, crushed

1 tsp paprika

1 tbsp ground cumin

1 cup 1 cup (250ml, 8fl oz) sweet chilli sauce

STAPLES

3 tbsps olive oil

Freshly ground salt and pepper

¼ cup (60ml, 2fl oz) water

OPTIONAL

2 large Lebanese cucumbers, sliced

1 cup (15g, ½ oz) mint leaves

1 tbsp chilli flakes, to garnish

Place the lamb, onion, garlic, paprika and a couple of grinds of salt and pepper in a bowl and mix to thoroughly combine. Form into golf-ball-sized meatballs.

Heat the oil in a large, deep-sided frying pan over medium-high heat. Fry the meatballs in batches for 12 minutes, turning every 2 minutes until cooked through.

Return all the meatballs to the pan, mix the cumin with the chilli sauce and water and add to pan. Cook for 10 minutes, turning the meatballs to coat in the sauce.

To serve, arrange the cucumbers and mint leaves on serving plates, place the meatballs over the top and drizzle over remaining sauce and sprinkle the chilli flakes over the top.

1 HR

Beef Kofte in Curry Sauce

800g (1¾ lb) minced beef

4 large onions, grated and squeezed to remove excess liquid

4 tbsps fresh ginger, minced

3 tbsps garam masala

6 cloves garlic, crushed

1 tbsp ground cumin

STAPLES

¼ cup (60ml, 2fl oz) olive oil

Freshly ground salt and pepper

2 cups (500ml, 1pt) water (or vegetable stock)

OPTIONAL

1 cup (250ml, 8fl oz) Greek yoghurt, to serve

Place the beef, a third of the onions, half each of the ginger, garam masala and garlic, along with the cumin and 1 teaspoon each of salt and pepper in a bowl and mix together. Form into small 5cm (2in) long sausages.

Heat the oil in a large heavy-bottomed saucepan over medium heat. Fry the rest of the onions and garlic for 5 minutes. Add the rest of the ginger and garam masala and saute another minute. Increase heat to medium-high and fry the kofte in batches for 8 minutes.

Return all the koftes to the pan, along with the water. Bring to a boil. Reduce the heat to low, cover and simmer for 30 minutes.

Just before serving, if desired stir through half the yoghurt, and dollop the rest on top.

2 HR

1.5

CUPS

Beetroot Hummus

2 large beetroots, washed and dried

1 x 400g (14oz) can chickpeas, drained and rinsed

3 tbsps tahini paste

4 small cloves garlic, skin on

1½ tbsps lemon juice

1 tsp ground coriander

STAPLES

2 tbsps olive oil

Freshly ground salt and pepper

OPTIONAL

2 tbsps pine nuts, to garnish

1 tbsp parsley, finely chopped, to garnish

1 tbsp sesame seeds, to garnish

½ tsp nigella seeds, to garnish

Preheat the oven to 200°C (400°F, Gas Mark 6).

Place the beetroots and two cloves garlic each in the middle of two large foil squares. Drizzle them with the olive oil then wrap up completely in the foil. Roast for 1 ½ hours until the beetroots are tender.

Let them cool for 20 minutes then remove the skins. Roughly chop and place in a food processor along with the garlic flesh. Add the chickpeas, tahini, half the lemon juice, coriander, and salt and pepper to taste.

Puree until you have a smooth paste. Add more lemon juice to taste and a small amount of water to thin it out if needed. Serve garnished with pine nuts, parsley, sesame and nigella seeds.

40 MIN

Rose Water and Raspberry Puffs

8 sheets filo pastry

1½ cups (335g, 12oz) mascarpone

¼ cup (60ml, 2fl oz) rose water

1 tsp lemon juice

3 cups (375g, 13oz) fresh raspberries

1 cup (15g, ½ oz) mint leaves

STAPLES

¼ cup (60ml, 2fl oz) vegetable oil

2 tbsps caster sugar

OPTIONAL

¼ cup (40g, 1½ oz) icing sugar

Preheat the oven to 180°C (350°F, Gas Mark 4) and lightly oil two 6-hole cupcake tins

Whisk together the mascarpone, rose water, lemon juice and caster sugar and set aside.

Cut the filo sheets into 10cm (4in) squares and layer 3 squares into each cup, lightly brushing the top with oil. Push them into the cups, cover with a square of foil and weigh each down with baking beads.

Bake for 13 minutes until they're golden brown. Remove from the oven and carefully remove the beads and foil.

Place a dollop of rose water mascarpone in each cup, top with fresh raspberries and if desired dust icing sugar over the top. Decorate with fresh mint leaves.

1 HR

6

Lebanese Pudding

⅔ cup (100g, 4oz) short-grain rice

½ cup (115g, 4oz) mascarpone

1½ tbsps rose water

1 cup (125g, 4oz) pistachios, chopped

STAPLES

1 cup (250ml, 8fl oz) water

3 cups (750ml, 24fl oz) full cream milk

2 tbsps arrowroot flour

⅓ cup (70g, 2½ oz) caster sugar

Rinse the rice until the water runs clear. Place in a large, heavy-bottomed saucepan with the cup of water and bring to a boil. Reduce to low and simmer for 8 minutes.

Whisk together arrowroot flour with 3 tablespoons of milk in a large bowl, then whisk in the rest of the milk, the mascarpone, rose water and sugar.

Add the mixture to the rice and bring to a boil, then again reduce the heat to low and simmer for 30 minutes or until the rice is tender and cooked through. Stir frequently to ensure it doesn't burn or stick to the bottom of the pot.

Serve the pudding warm, topped with pistachios.

turkish

15 MIN

CUPS

White Bean Dip

2 x 400g (14oz) cans cannellini beans, drained and rinsed

2½ tbsps tahini paste

2 small cloves garlic, roughly chopped

½ cup (125ml, 4fl oz) lemon juice

STAPLES

2 tbsps olive oil

Freshly ground salt and pepper

Place the beans, tahini paste, garlic, half the lemon juice, 1 tablespoon of oil and a couple of grinds of salt in a food processor or blender and puree until smooth. Add more lemon juice to taste.

Serve the dip with the remaining olive oil drizzled over and freshly ground pepper over the top.

4

Menemen

½ large green capsicum, finely chopped

1 large onion, chopped

110g (4oz) sucuk or mild salami, chopped

1 x 400g (14oz) can diced tomatoes

½ cup (115g, 4oz) tomato passata

⅓ cup (80ml, 3fl oz) Greek yoghurt

STAPLES

1 tbsp olive oil

½ tsp sugar

3 small eggs

Freshly ground salt and pepper

OPTIONAL

Fresh parsley leaves, to garnish

Heat the oil in a large, deep-sided frying pan over medium-high heat. Fry the onions for 3 minutes, add the capsicum and sucuk and cook for a further 3 minutes. Add the tomatoes, passata and sugar. Cook for 15 minutes until the sauce has thickened slightly.

Break the eggs into the mix and gently stir through. Once they have cooked, season to taste with salt and pepper.

Serve hot drizzled with yoghurt and garnished with parsley.

1 HR

4

Gozleme

1 x 7g (¼ oz) sachet dried yeast

200g (7oz) Greek feta, crumbled

5 cups (150g, 5oz) baby spinach, roughly chopped

⅔ cup (160ml, 5fl oz) Greek yoghurt

1 lemon, cut into wedges

1 tsp sumac

STAPLES

Freshly ground salt and pepper

1 tsp caster sugar

1¼ cups (280ml, 9fl oz) warm water

3¼ cups (405g, 14oz) plain flour

⅓ cup (90ml, 3fl oz) vegetable oil

Gently stir together the yeast, a pinch of salt, sugar and warm water in a small bowl. Set aside for 5 minutes.

Place 3 cups of flour in a large bowl and make a well in the middle. Pour the yeast mixture into the middle and mix together to form a dough. Use some of the extra flour to dust a work surface. Turn out the dough and knead for 5 minutes, then divide into four pieces. Place them on a lightly oiled tray, cover with plastic wrap and let them sit for 30 minutes.

Roll out each piece into a large 30 x 50cm (12 x 20in) rectangle. Spread half of each rectangle with equal amounts of feta and spinach and sprinkle over a pinch of sumac and a couple of grinds of salt and pepper. Fold the dough over and seal at the edges.

Heat a large frying pan over medium-high heat. Brush the gozlemes with oil and fry on each side for 3 minutes until browned.

Serve cut into fifths with yoghurt and lemon wedges on the side.

**10 MIN
+ SOAKING**

Kisir

1 cup (180g, 6oz) bulgur

1 small Continental cucumber, chopped

¼ cup (10g, ¼ oz) fresh parsley, finely chopped

¼ cup (10g, ¼ oz) fresh mint, finely chopped

2 tbsps tomato paste

¼ cup (50ml, 2fl oz) lemon juice

STAPLES

2½ tbsps olive oil

Freshly ground salt and pepper

1½ cups (375ml, 13fl oz) hot water (or use vegetable stock)

OPTIONAL

2 spring onions, chopped

Rinse the bulgur then place in a large bowl with the hot water (or stock if using). Cover with a tea towel and let sit for 30 minutes. Drain the bulgur then place in a clean tea towel and squeeze it tightly to remove excess liquid. Place in a large salad bowl.

Add the tomato paste, half the lemon juice, the oil and a couple of grinds of salt and pepper to the bulgur and mix together thoroughly.

Stir through the cucumber, herbs and spring onions, if using, and add more lemon juice to taste and season further with salt and pepper.

Serve.

40 MIN

25 ROLLS

Crispy Cheese Boreks

375g (13oz) filo pastry

300g (10oz) Greek feta cheese, crumbled

6 large spring onions, finely chopped

3 cloves garlic, crushed

3 tbsps sesame seeds, lightly toasted

1 tsp ground cumin

STAPLES

Vegetable oil, for frying

2 large eggs, lightly beaten

Freshly ground salt and pepper

OPTIONAL

1 pinch cayenne pepper

Mix together the feta, spring onions, garlic, half the sesame seeds, cumin, eggs, cayenne (if using) and a couple of grinds of salt and pepper.

Dampen two tea towels and keep the filo pastry between them. Cut a sheet of filo in half lengthwise. Place 2 tablespoons of mixture near the end of one piece, leaving a 2cm (1in) border on each side. Fold over the sides and roll up the filo, using a dab of water to seal the end.

Repeat with the other half and the rest of the filo sheets until you've used up all the filling.

Heat 1cm (½ in) of oil in a large, deep-sided frying pan. Fry the boreks for 4 minutes, turning frequently until golden brown. Drain on paper towels and serve hot, garnished with the remaining sesame seeds.

Saksuka Meze

2 eggplants, cut into 1½ cm (¾ in) cubes

2 small zucchinis, cut into 1½ cm (¾ in) cubes

1 x 400g (14oz) can diced tomatoes

1 onion, quartered and sliced

2 cloves garlic, crushed

1½ tbsps tomato paste

STAPLES

Olive oil, for frying

1 tsp sugar

Freshly ground salt and pepper

OPTIONAL

1 yellow bullhorn pepper, roughly chopped

Fresh parsley leaves, to garnish

Heat 2cm (1in) oil in a large deep-sided frying pan over medium-high heat. Fry the eggplant in batches for at least 6 minutes or until the eggplant is beginning to brown on the edges. Remove the eggplant with a slotted spoon and drain on paper towels. Repeat with the zucchini.

Heat 1 ½ tablespoons of oil in a frying pan over medium heat. Fry the onion and garlic for 5 minutes. Add the tomato paste and fry for 1 minute.

Add the tomatoes, sugar and bullhorn pepper, if using. Bring to a boil then reduce to low and simmer, covered, for 20 minutes.

Place the eggplant, zucchini and tomato sauce in a large bowl, toss, season to taste then chill in the refrigerator for at least 4 hours. Serve cold, garnished with parsley.

45 MIN

4

Bean Stew

2 small onions, chopped

3 small cloves garlic, crushed

1 large carrot, finely chopped

2 x 400g (14oz) cans kidney beans, drained and rinsed

1 x 400g (14oz) can diced tomatoes

2 cups (500ml, 1pt) beef stock

STAPLES

2 tbsps olive oil

1 tsp sugar

Freshly ground salt and pepper

OPTIONAL

1 tbsp lemon juice

1 tsp sweet paprika

Heat the oil in a large, heavy-bottomed frying pan over medium heat. Fry the onions and garlic for 5 minutes.

Add the carrot and fry for another 5 minutes, then add the kidney beans, tomatoes, stock and sugar, and lemon juice and paprika, if using. Bring to a boil, then reduce the heat to low and simmer, covered, for 30 minutes.

Season to taste and serve hot.

25 MIN
+ RESTING

Za'atar Pizza

¾ tsp dried yeast

¾ cup (185ml, 6fl oz) Greek yoghurt (room temperature)

1 double amount za'atar spice mix (see recipe page 148)

STAPLES

2 cups (250g, 8oz) plain flour (use bread flour if possible)

1 tsp salt

2 tsps sugar

4 tbsps olive oil

Place the flour, salt, yeast and sugar in a large bowl and stir to mix through. Add 2 tablespoons of olive oil and the yoghurt and mix together until it forms a dough.

Turn out onto a lightly floured surface and knead for 10 minutes. Place in an oiled container and sit, covered with plastic wrap, in a warm place for 2 hours.

Cut the dough into 6 equal pieces, roll into balls and let them sit, covered, with a damp cloth for a further 2 hours.

Preheat oven to 250°C (475°F, Gas Mark 9). Roll out into 1cm (½ in) thick rounds and place on an oiled baking tray. Bake for 5 minutes, then flip them over, brush with oil and spread the za'atar mix over the top.

Bake for another 5 minutes until cooked through. Serve hot.

1 HR, 15 MIN

4

Manti Dumplings

400g (14oz) minced lamb

1 onion, grated and squeezed to remove excess liquid

2 small cloves garlic, minced

2 tsps sweet paprika

2 tbsps tomato paste

1 cup (250ml, 8fl oz) Greek yoghurt

STAPLES

2 cups (250g, 8oz) plain flour

1 tsp salt

2 small eggs, lightly whisked

1¼ cups (310ml, 10fl oz) water

2 tbsps olive oil

Freshly ground salt and pepper

OPTIONAL

1 tbsp chilli flakes, to garnish

2 tsps dried mint, to garnish

Place the flour and salt in a bowl. Add eggs and ½ cup water. Mix until it forms a dough.

Knead for 10 minutes on a lightly floured surface. Place in an oiled container, covered, in the refrigerator for 25 minutes.

Mix together the onion, lamb, half the garlic and half the paprika, and a couple of grinds of salt and pepper and set aside.

Halve the dough, keep half in the bowl, covered, and roll out the other on a lightly floured surface as thin as you can. Cut into 5cm (2in) squares and place ½ tablespoon of filling on the centre of each. Fold up the dough and pinch at the top to seal. Transfer to a floured plate and sprinkle with flour to keep them from sticking together. Repeat with the rest of the dough and filling.

Heat the oil in a small saucepan over medium heat and fry the remaining garlic for 1 minute. Add the remaining paprika, the tomato paste and ¾ cup water. Bring to a boil, then simmer for 10 minutes. Set aside.

Bring a large pot of salted water to the boil and boil the dumplings for 20 minutes. Drain and serve with the yoghurt and sauce drizzled over the top, garnished with dried mint and chilli flakes.

Kibbeh with Lamb and Pine Nuts

2½ cups (450g, 1lb) bulgur

1kg (2lb) minced lamb

2 onions; 1 grated and squeezed to remove excess liquid, 1 chopped

1½ tsps allspice

1½ tsps ground oregano

½ cup (70g, 2½ oz) pine nuts

STAPLES

2½ tbsps olive oil

Freshly ground salt and pepper

Vegetable oil, for frying

OPTIONAL

Greek yoghurt, to serve

Place the bulgur in a large heatproof bowl and cover with boiling water. Leave to soak for 30 minutes. Drain, then place the bulgur in a clean tea towel and use it to squeeze out any excess water.

Mix together the bulgur, 600g (1lb 5oz) lamb, grated onion, 1 teaspoon allspice, 1 teaspoon oregano, 1 tablespoon olive oil, some grinds of salt and pepper and a dash of water. Set aside.

Heat the rest of the oil in a large frying pan over medium heat and fry the chopped onion and the pine nuts for 5 minutes. Add the rest of the lamb, allspice, oregano and some grinds of salt and pepper and fry for 7 minutes until the lamb is browned. Let cool for 20 minutes.

Form the uncooked mixture into egg-shapes and make a large hole in each one. Fill the holes with the cooked filling and seal over.

Heat 1cm (½ in) vegetable oil in a large deep-sided frying pan and fry the kibbeh in batches for 10 minutes, turning frequently to cook all over. Drain on paper towels and serve hot with yoghurt on the side.

**1 HR
+ CHILLING**

 4

Turkish Bean Salad

300g (10oz)
green beans, ends
trimmed

600g (1lb 5oz)
yellow beans, ends
trimmed

1 small onion, finely
chopped

2 large cloves
garlic, sliced

1 x 400g (14oz) can
diced tomatoes,
drained

1½ tsps paprika

STAPLES

2 tbsps olive oil

1 cup (250ml, 8fl
oz) water

1 tsp sugar

Freshly ground salt
and pepper

Shave along the sides of the beans using a
sharp knife.

Heat the oil in a large saucepan over medium
heat and fry the onion for 5 minutes.

Add the rest of the ingredients. Bring to a
boil then reduce the heat to low.

Cover and simmer for 40 minutes, adding
more water as needed.

Season to taste, then let it cool for at least
1 hour, then chill in the refrigerator for at
least 4 hours.

Serve cold.

Herb Kofta
with Flatbreads

1kg (2lb) minced beef

½ onion, grated

2 cloves garlic, crushed

2 tbsps dried mixed herbs

¼ cup (10g, ¼ oz) fresh mint leaves, finely chopped

6 Turkish flatbreads

STAPLES

1 tbsp olive oil plus extra for frying

½ tbsp salt

½ tbsp freshly ground pepper

OPTIONAL

Fresh parsley leaves, to garnish

¾ cup (185ml, 6fl oz) Greek yoghurt, to serve

Mix together all the ingredients, except the parsley and yoghurt, in a large bowl.

Divide the mixture into 12 equal portions and mould into thick short sausage shapes.

Heat 1cm (½ in) oil in a deep-sided frying pan and fry the kofte in batches for 12 minutes, turning frequently until cooked through.

Brush the flatbreads with oil and fry for 1 minute each side.

Serve the kofte warm with the flatbreads. If desired serve yoghurt on the side and garnish with parsley.

Pide Pizza

1 batch flatbread dough (see recipe page 173)

1 large onion, finely chopped

600g (1lb 5oz) minced lamb

1 x 400g (14oz) can diced tomatoes, drained

2 tsps sumac

2 tsps ground cumin

STAPLES

2 tbsps olive oil

Freshly ground salt and pepper

OPTIONAL

2 small cloves garlic, crushed

2 tsps ground coriander

Fresh parsley, roughly chopped, to serve

Preheat the oven to 250°C (475°F, Gas Mark 9) and lightly oil a large deep-sided baking tray.

Roll the dough out to slightly larger than the tray, gently push into the tray, letting the sides sit up slightly. Cover with a damp tea towel and let it rise in a warm place for 30 minutes.

Heat the oil in a large frying pan over medium heat and fry the onion (and garlic, if using) for 5 minutes. Add the sumac and cumin (and coriander, if using) and fry for 1 minute then add the lamb and fry for another 5 minutes until just browned.

Add the tomatoes and cook for 10 more minutes. Season to taste. Let cool slightly.

Spread the lamb mix out over the pizza base.

Bake for 15 minutes until the crust is browned and cooked through.

Serve the pizza hot with parsley sprinkled over the top.

Meatballs in Egg Lemon Sauce

600g (1lb 5oz) minced lamb

⅔ cup (30g, 1oz) parsley, chopped (reserve 2 tbsps for garnish)

¼ cup (40g, 1½ oz) long-grain rice

2 lemons, juiced

3 tbsps dill (fresh or dried)

1 tsp ground coriander

STAPLES

3 cups (700ml, 24fl oz) water

2 large eggs, lightly beaten

1½ tbsps flour

Freshly ground salt and pepper

Mix together the lamb, parsley, rice, dill and coriander and form into golf-ball-sized meatballs. Let them chill in the refrigerator for at least 20 minutes.

Bring the water to the boil in a large pot. Reduce to a simmer and place the meatballs in water. Simmer, covered, for 25 minutes. There should always be just enough water to cover the meatballs.

Whisk together the eggs, flour and lemon juice. Pour ¼ cup of the hot water from the meatballs into the egg mixture and whisk to mix thoroughly.

Stir the egg mix into the meatball mix and cook for 6 more minutes but don't let it boil.

Season to taste and serve sprinkled with the remaining parsley.

**55 MIN
+ COOLING**

Baby Broad
Bean Salad

500g (1lb) baby broad beans, unpodded, ends trimmed, cut into 3cm (1in) lengths

1 onion, chopped

2½ tbsps lemon juice

2 Roma tomatoes, seeded and chopped

½ cup (20g, ¾ oz) fresh dill, roughly chopped

3 small cloves garlic, crushed

STAPLES

3 tsps plain flour

½ cup (140ml, 5fl oz) water

⅓ cup (80ml, 3fl oz) extra virgin olive oil

Whisk together the flour, water and lemon juice. Soak the beans in this mixture for 10 minutes.

Heat the oil in a large, deep-sided frying pan over medium heat and fry the onion for 5 minutes. Add the garlic and fry for 1 minute. Add the tomatoes and fry for another 2 minutes. Add the beans and accompanying flour mixture and stir through.

Sprinkle over a couple of grinds of salt and pepper. Turn the heat down to low and cook for 20 minutes. Add water as needed to stop the mixture from drying out. Mix through half the dill and cook for a further 5 minutes.

Remove from the heat and let cool to room temperature for 1 hour. Serve garnished with the remaining dill.

4

Cacik

3 cups (750ml, 24fl oz) Greek yoghurt

2 small Lebanese cucumbers, chopped

2 large cloves garlic, crushed

½ tbsp fresh dill, finely chopped

STAPLES

1 cup (250ml, 8fl oz) filtered water

1 tsp salt

OPTIONAL

Fresh mint leaves, to garnish

Whisk together the yoghurt and water.

Stir through the cucumbers, garlic, dill and salt, ensuring everything is well combined.

Season further to taste and serve garnished with mint leaves.

40 MIN

Okra with Tomatoes

500g (1lb) okra, rinsed

2 onions, chopped

4 small cloves garlic, crushed

1 x 400g (14oz) can diced tomatoes

½ cup (115g, 4oz) tomato passata

¼ cup (60ml, 2fl oz) lemon juice

STAPLES

¼ cup (50ml, 2fl oz) olive oil

¼ tsp sugar

½ cup (125ml, 4fl oz) water

Freshly ground salt and pepper

OPTIONAL

1½ tbsps ground oregano

Heat the oil in a large, deep-sided saucepan over medium heat. Fry the onion for 5 minutes, then add the okra and garlic and fry for a further minute.

Stir through the oregano, if using, then add the tomatoes, passata and sugar. Add the lemon juice and water and bring to a boil, then reduce heat to low and simmer for 25 minutes.

Once the okra is cooked through, season to taste and serve hot.

1 HR

Stuffed Pumpkin

6 dumpling or
golden nugget
pumpkins

2½ cups (465g, 1lb)
cooked quinoa

6 large spring
onions, chopped

¾ cup (100g,
3½ oz) pine nuts,
chopped

3 tsps dried chilli
flakes

200g (7oz)
mozzarella cheese,
grated or cut into
thick slices

STAPLES

⅓ cup (100ml, 3½
fl oz) olive oil

Freshly ground salt
and pepper

OPTIONAL

1 tbsp ground
oregano

Preheat the oven to 200°C (400°F, Gas Mark 6) and line two
large baking trays with baking paper.

Slice the tops off the pumpkins so they make a lid and scoop
out the seeds and threads.

Place the pumpkins on the trays (thinly slice the bottoms if
needed to help them sit flat). Rub them with 3 tablespoons
of the oil and lightly season with salt and pepper. Roast for
20 minutes, then remove and let them cool.

Scoop out the flesh, leaving 1cm (½ in) of flesh still in the
pumpkins, and mix the flesh through the quinoa.

Heat the rest of the oil in a large frying pan over medium
heat and fry the spring onion for 5 minutes. Add the pine
nuts and 2 teaspoons of chilli as well as the ground oregano,
if using, and stir for 2 minutes. Add the quinoa mix and heat
through. Season to taste, then stuff the pumpkins with the
mixture flush with the edges.

Gently place the mozzarella on top the mixture and put the
lids over the top. Bake for 20 minutes until the pumpkins are
soft and the cheese is melted.

Rice and Lentils with Crispy Onions

1 large onion, quartered and sliced

4 cups (650g, 1lb 7oz) cooked long-grain rice

2 cups (400g, 14oz) cooked brown lentils

Seeds from 1 large pomegranate

3 cloves garlic, crushed

1 tbsp ground cumin

STAPLES

⅔ cup (150ml, 5fl oz) plus 1 tbsp olive oil

Freshly ground salt and pepper

1 tbsp cornflour

OPTIONAL

1 tsp ground coriander

½ tsp allspice

Toss the onion slices in the cornflour to lightly coat.

Heat the ⅔ cup oil in a small frying pan over medium heat. Fry the onion for 15 minutes, until golden and just crisp. Drain on paper towels and set aside.

Heat the 1 tablespoon oil in a large deep-sided frying pan over medium heat. Fry the garlic and cumin, with coriander and allspice, if using, for 1 minute. Add the rice, lentils and a few grinds of salt and pepper and mix through.

Reduce the heat to low and gently heat through.

Remove the rice mixture from the pan, toss the pomegranate seeds through and top with the fried onions.

4

Fish and Potato Stew

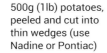

500g (1lb) potatoes, peeled and cut into thin wedges (use Nadine or Pontiac)

4 x 100g (3½ oz) white fish fillets, skin on, patted dry.

1 cup (250g, 9oz) cherry tomatoes, halved

3 cloves garlic, crushed

2 cups (500ml, 1pt) vegetable stock

2 tbsps ras el hanout

STAPLES

¼ cup (60ml, 2fl oz) olive oil

Freshly ground salt and pepper

OPTIONAL

¼ cup (10g, ¼ oz) fresh parsley, chopped

Heat 2 tablespoons oil in a large, heavy-based casserole dish over medium heat. Fry the potatoes, garlic and half the spice mix for 3 minutes. Add the tomatoes and cook for 5 more minutes. Add the stock and bring to a boil. Reduce to a simmer for 15 minutes.

Rub the remaining spice mix into the fish. Heat remaining oil in a separate frying pan over medium heat and fry the fish, skin down, for 4 minutes until the skin is crisp. Carefully remove and place in the stew.

Simmer for another 15 minutes until the fish is cooked through and the potato is tender. Stir through half the parsley, season to taste and serve with the remaining parsley scattered over the top.

2 HR

Stuffed Eggplant

4 large eggplants, halved lengthways.

2 large onions, quartered and sliced

8 Roma tomatoes, peeled and chopped

3 cloves garlic, crushed

1 tbsps ras el hanout

1 cup (45g, 1½ oz) fresh parsley, chopped

STAPLES

¼ cup (60ml, 2fl oz) olive oil

Freshly ground salt and pepper

¼ tsp sugar

OPTIONAL

1 tbsp lemon juice

Preheat oven to 150°C (300°F, Gas Mark 2).

Brush the eggplant halves with half the oil and dust with salt and pepper. Bake them in the oven, cut side down, for 15 minutes. Remove and let cool.

Scoop out the filling, leaving 1cm (½ in) of flesh attached to the skin. Roughly chop the flesh and set aside.

Heat the remaining oil in a large frying pan over medium heat. Fry the onion for 5 minutes, then add the garlic and spice mix and fry for another 2 minutes.

Add the tomatoes, half the parsley, sugar and eggplant flesh, and add the lemon juice if using. Let it simmer on low for 25 minutes. Season to taste.

Stuff the eggplants with the filling and place them snugly in a shallow baking dish. Cover with foil and bake for 45 minutes.

Serve hot or cold garnished with the remaining parsley.

50 MIN

4

Fellah Koftes

1 cup (180g, 6oz)
bulgur

½ cup (85g, 3oz)
fine semolina

1½ tbsps tomato
paste

½ tbsp ras el
hanout mix

4 large Roma
tomatoes, finely
chopped

2 tbsps
pomegranate
molasses

STAPLES

1⅓ cups (350ml,
(12fl oz) plus 8 cups
(2L, 4pt) water

1 egg, lightly beaten

½ cup (60g, 2oz)
plain flour

⅓ cup (80ml, 3fl oz)
olive oil

Freshly ground salt
and pepper

OPTIONAL

2 tbsps fresh dill,
chopped, to garnish

¼ cup (10g, ¼ oz)
fresh parsley,
chopped, to garnish

Greek yoghurt, to
serve

Simmer the bulgur, semolina and 1⅓ cups water in a large pot until the water is absorbed. Let cool for 20 minutes, then mix through the egg, flour, ½ tablespoon tomato paste and the spice mix.

Form the mix into golf-ball-sized balls, slightly flatten them and make little indents in the middle, then set aside.

Heat the oil in a frying pan over medium heat and fry the remaining tomato paste for 1 minute. Add the chopped tomatoes and cook for 10 minutes. Stir through ½ teaspoon salt and the molasses. Season further to taste then turn off the heat.

Boil 8 cups of water in a large pot and boil the koftes in small batches. Once they rise to the surface, they should be cooked.

Serve the koftes with the sauce drizzled over and sprinkled with dill and parsley, and with the yoghurt on the side for dipping, if desired.

30 MIN

Barbecue Kofte

1kg (2lb) chicken mince

½ onion, grated

2 cloves garlic, crushed

1 tbsp ground cumin

1 tbsp ground oregano

1 tsps ground coriander

12 metal skewers

STAPLES

1 tbsp olive oil

2 tsps salt

2 tsps freshly ground pepper

Mix together all the ingredients in a large bowl.

Divide the mixture into 12 equal portions and mould each one around a skewer like a sausage.

Heat a barbecue grill over medium-high heat.

Grill the koftes for 8 minutes, turning every 2 minutes until browned and cooked through.

Serve hot.

15 MIN

Bean and Dill Salad

2 x 400g (14oz) cans black-eyed beans, drained and rinsed

4 spring onions, thinly sliced

4 large Roma tomatoes, seeded and finely chopped

½ cup (20g, ¾ oz) fresh parsley, finely chopped

½ cup (20g, ¾ oz) fresh dill, finely chopped

½ cup (125ml, 4fl oz) lemon juice

STAPLES

½ cup (110ml, 4fl oz) olive oil

Freshly ground salt and pepper

OPTIONAL

1 small green capsicum, finely chopped

Place the beans, spring onion, tomato, parsley, dill and capsicum, if using, in a large bowl.

Whisk together the lemon juice, oil and a few good grinds of salt and pepper.

Pour over the salad mix and toss to combine.

Serve.

Cevapcici with Baked Potatoes

800g (1¾ lb) minced beef

4 large cloves garlic, crushed

2 onions, grated and squeezed to remove excess liquid

1½ tbsps smoked paprika

¼ tsp cayenne pepper

500g (1lb) potatoes, peeled and cut into large chunks for roasting (Use Dutch Cream or Nicola)

STAPLES

Freshly ground salt and pepper

2 tbsps olive oil

1 tbsp butter

⅓ cup (80ml, 3fl oz) vegetable oil

OPTIONAL

Salad, to serve

Greek yoghurt, to serve

Mix together the beef, half the garlic, the onion, paprika, cayenne and a few good grinds of salt and pepper in a large bowl then cover and refrigerate for 3 hours.

Half an hour before the meat mix is ready to use, steam the potatoes for 10 minutes until they're slightly softened on the outside.

Preheat the oven to 200°C (400°F, Gas Mark 6).

Toss the potatoes with the rest of the garlic, the olive oil, 2 teaspoons salt and the butter. Place on a roasting tray and roast for 40 minutes until crisp and just browned on the outside.

Separate the meat into 12 portions and roll them into thick sausage shapes.

Heat the vegetable oil in a frying pan over medium-high heat and cook the cevapcicis for 12 minutes, turning every 2 minutes.

Serve the cevapcicis hot with the roasted potatoes, and salad and yoghurt for dipping on the side, if desired.

1 HR, 40 MINS

Eggplant Capsicum Parsley Sauce

2 large eggplants, halved lengthways

3 large cloves garlic, skin on

1 small onion, finely chopped

½ tbsp fresh ginger, minced

½ red capsicum, finely chopped

⅔ cup (30g, 1oz) fresh parsley, finely chopped

STAPLES

⅓ cup (80ml, 3fl oz) olive oil

Freshly ground salt and pepper

OPTIONAL

1 green chilli, seeded and finely chopped

1 tsp ground cumin

1 tsp ground oregano

Preheat oven to 180°C (350°F, Gas Mark 4) and line a large flat baking tray with baking paper.

Brush the eggplants lightly with oil and bake in the oven for 40 minutes until darkened on the outside and soft. Brush the garlic with oil and add to the oven for the last 20 minutes.

Place the eggplants and garlic in a sealed container and let them cool for 30 minutes.

Peel the skin from the eggplant and garlic and roughly chop both. Place the flesh in a large mixing bowl and set aside.

Heat the rest of the oil in a frying pan over medium heat and fry the onion for 6 minutes. Add the ginger and if using, the chilli, cumin and oregano, and fry for 2 more minutes. Place in the bowl with the chopped eggplant and garlic.

Use a potato masher to mash up the mix into a thick paste. Stir through the capsicum and parsley.

Season to taste and serve.

Turkish Meatballs

1kg (2lb) minced beef

½ cup (60g, 2oz) fresh breadcrumbs

2 large onions, grated and squeezed to remove excess liquid

3 large cloves garlic, crushed

1 tbsp ras el hanout

½ cup (20g, ¾ oz) fresh parsley, finely chopped

STAPLES

2 small eggs, lightly beaten

1 tsp salt

2 tsps freshly ground pepper

⅓ cup (70ml, 2½ fl oz) olive oil

OPTIONAL

1 pinch cayenne pepper

1 tsp lemon juice

Place all the ingredients except the oil in a bowl and mix together. Knead like a dough for 5 minutes. Cover and place in the refrigerator for at least 1 hour.

Preheat the oven to 180°C (350°F, Gas Mark 4) and line two large baking trays with baking paper.

Form the mix into mini burger patties, around 5cm (2in) wide and 1cm (½ in) thick.

Place them on the trays and lightly brush with the olive oil.

Bake for 25 minutes, then turn them over and bake for a further 15 minutes.

Serve hot.

15 MIN

4

Piyaz Bean Salad

2 x 400g (14oz)
cans butter beans,
drained and rinsed

1 large white onion,
quartered and sliced

2 bird's-eye chillies,
seeded and finely
chopped

¼ cup (60ml, 2fl oz)
lemon juice

½ cup (20g, ¾ oz)
fresh parsley,
chopped and tightly
packed

2 small cloves
garlic, crushed

STAPLES

¼ cup (60ml, 2fl oz)
olive oil

Freshly ground salt
and pepper

Place the beans, onion, chillies and parsley
in a large salad bowl and gently mix
through.

Whisk together the lemon juice, garlic, oil
and a couple of grinds of salt and pepper.
Drizzle over the salad and then gently toss
to combine.

Season the salad further to taste and serve.

30 MIN
+ MARINATING

Lamb Kebabs with Pomegranate Molasses

700g (1½ lb) lamb leg, cut into 2cm (1in) cubes

6 tablespoons pomegranate molasses (or use hoisin sauce), divided

½ onion, grated

1 tbsp dried oregano

12 Asian shallots, cut in half

8 wooden skewers, soaked in hot water for 30 minutes

STAPLES

1 tsp salt

1 tsp freshly ground pepper

Combine 3 tablespoons of pomegranate molasses, the grated onion, oregano, salt and pepper in a large zip-lock bag. Add the lamb and rub to coat thoroughly. Place in the fridge to marinate for at least 1 hour and up to 8 hours.

When ready to cook, thread the cubes of lamb and the shallots onto the skewers.

Heat a barbecue to medium heat.

Grill the kebabs for 12 minutes, turning and brushing with pomegranate molasses every 3 minutes, until cooked through and slightly charred on the outside. Pour any remaining molasses evenly over the kebabs to serve.

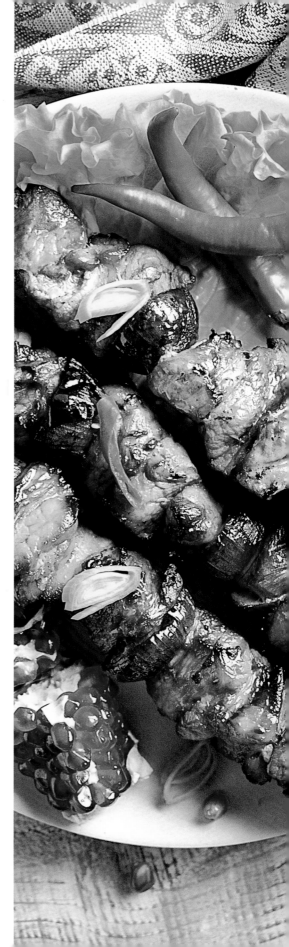

15 MIN

Gavurdagi

6 large tomatoes, seeded and chopped

1 large onion, chopped

1½ cups (185g, 6oz) walnuts, roughly chopped

⅔ cup (30g, 1oz) parsley, roughly chopped

¼ cup (50ml, 2fl oz) pomegranate molasses

1 tbsp ras el hanout

STAPLES

¼ cup (60ml, 2fl oz) olive oil

Freshly ground salt and pepper

Place the tomato, onion, walnuts and parsley in a large salad bowl and toss to combine.

Whisk together the molasses, spice mix, oil and a couple of grinds of salt and pepper.

Drizzle over the salad and mix through. Season further to taste and serve.

**50 MIN
+ MARINATING**

Baked Spiced Chicken

800g (1¾ lb)
chicken breast
fillets, cut into 2cm
(1in) chunks

1 large onion,
grated and
squeezed to remove
excess liquid

½ cup (125ml,
4fl oz) Greek
yoghurt

¼ cup (60g, 2oz)
tomato passata

¼ cup (60ml, 2fl oz)
lemon juice

2 tsps ras el hanout

STAPLES

⅓ cup (70ml, 2½ fl
oz) olive oil

Freshly ground salt
and pepper

OPTIONAL

2 large cloves
garlic, crushed

Whisk together all the ingredients except the chicken and add
a couple of grinds of salt and pepper.

Pour over the chicken and coat thoroughly, cover, then
marinate in the refrigerator for 4 hours, preferably overnight.

Preheat oven to 220°C (425°F, Gas Mark 7) and line two large
baking trays with baking paper.

Place the chicken pieces on the trays, leaving spaces between
each chunk so they don't touch.

Bake for 15 minutes, then take them out of the oven, turn
and drizzle with a small amount of olive oil. Bake for a further
15 minutes until browned.

Season further to taste and serve hot.

1 HR, 10 MIN

16

PIECES

Baklava

3 cups (375g, 13oz) walnuts, finely chopped

Preheat oven to 180°C (350°F, Gas Mark 4) and grease a 18 x 28cm (7 x 11in) slice tin.

1 cup (125g, 4oz) pistachios, finely chopped

In a medium bowl, mix together the walnuts, half the pistachios, almonds, ½ cup sugar and the allspice, as well as the cardamom and cinnamon, if using.

½ cup (60g, 2oz) almonds, finely chopped

16 sheets filo pastry

Layer four sheets of the filo pastry in the slice tin, brushing each one with melted butter before placing the next one on top. Trim off any overhanging pastry. Spoon out a portion of the nut mixture and flatten with the back of the spoon before adding another layer of pastry. Repeat, until you have a top layer of pastry and all the nut mixture has been used up.

2 tbsps lemon juice

2 tsps allspice

STAPLES

125g (4oz) butter, melted, plus 1 tbsp room temp

Brush the top with the melted butter and cut the baklava into small rectangles with a sharp knife. You should end up with about 16. Bake for 25 minutes or until crisp and just turning golden.

½ cup (110g, 4oz) plus 1 tbsp caster sugar

½ cup (180g, 6oz) honey

To make the syrup, heat the tablespoons of butter and sugar, the honey and lemon juice in a medium saucepan over medium-high heat. Stir for 5 minutes until the sugar has dissolved and is boiling. Reduce to a simmer for a further 10 minutes until the mixture has thickened.

OPTIONAL

1 tsp ground cardamom

Pour the syrup over the slice and let it cool. Sprinkle the remaining pistachios over the top.

1 tsp cinnamon

20 MIN
+ CHILLING

Turkish Milk Pudding

¾ cup (90g, 3oz) walnuts, chopped

STAPLES

75g (3oz) unsalted butter

3½ tbsps plain flour

1 cup (220g, 8oz) sugar

3 cups (800ml, 27fl oz) milk

1 tsp vanilla extract

Heat the butter in a medium saucepan over medium heat. Once it starts to foam, add the flour and whisk for 1 minute.

Add the milk, ¼ cup at a time, whisking thoroughly to ensure there are no lumps, then stir in the sugar and vanilla. Stir until the pudding is thickened slightly and is almost boiling.

Remove from the heat, transfer into individual serving bowls and refrigerate overnight.

Serve sprinkled with walnuts.

1 HR, 30 MIN + CHIILING

25 PIECES

Turkish Delight

1½ tbsps lemon juice

¼ cup (30g, 1oz) arrowroot flour

1 tsp cream of tartar

1½ tbsps rose water

Red food colouring

STAPLES

1 tsp vegetable oil

4 cups (880g, 2lb) caster sugar

1⅓ cups (350ml, (12fl oz) plus 3 cups (730ml, 24fl oz) water

1 cup (150g, 5oz) cornflour

1 cup (155g, 5oz) icing sugar

Line a 23cm (9in) square slice tine with baking paper and lightly oil.

Heat the juice, caster sugar and 1⅓ cups water in a saucepan over medium heat, stirring until boiling. Reduce to low and let simmer until it reaches 115°C (240°F) on a candy thermometer. Remove from the heat.

Whisk together the arrowroot flour, cream of tartar, cornflour and 3 cups of water in another saucepan and bring to a boil, stirring constantly to prevent lumps forming. Once the mixture is gluey, add the lemon-sugar mixture. Simmer over low heat for just over 1 hour, stirring frequently to prevent lumps forming.

Stir in the rose water and a drop of food colouring. Pour into the prepared tin and let cool overnight. Cut into 2½ cm (1in) cubes and dust with the icing sugar.

spanish

20 MIN

Breaded Olives

40 large green
olives, pitted

1 cup (125g, 4oz)
breadcrumbs

½ tbsp smoked
paprika

½ tbsp ground
oregano

STAPLES

2 cups (250g, 8oz)
plain flour

2 tsps salt

4 large eggs, lightly
beaten

Vegetable oil, for
frying

Mix together the paprika, oregano, flour and
salt and place in a shallow dish.

Place the breadcrumbs and egg in separate
shallow dishes.

Coat the olives in the flour, shaking off any
excess, then the egg, shaking off excess,
then the breadcrumbs. Repeat with the
egg and breadcrumbs until all the olives are
coated thoroughly.

Heat 5cm (2in) oil in a deep-sided saucepan
over high heat. Fry the olives in small
batches for 3 minutes until just golden.

Drain on paper towels and serve hot.

20 MIN
+ CHILLING

Gazpacho

800g (1¾ lb) ripe tomatoes, seeded and roughly chopped

1 Lebanese cucumber, roughly chopped

1 large red capsicum, roughly chopped

4 small cloves garlic, crushed

1 small red onion, chopped

2½ cups (600ml, 21fl oz) tomato juice

STAPLES

3 tbsps extra virgin olive oil

3 tbsps apple cider vinegar

Freshly ground salt and pepper

OPTIONAL

1½ tbsps tomato paste

1 tsp ground cumin

Place the tomatoes, cucumber, capsicum and onion in a food processor and pulse a few times until they're chopped but still a bit chunky. Remove 2 cups' worth and set aside. Add the rest of the ingredients and puree until almost smooth.

Combine everything into a large container, cover and chill in the refrigerator for at least 4 hours, preferably overnight.

Season to taste and serve cold.

20 MIN

Garlic Prawns

800g (1¾ lb) prawn tails, shelled and veins removed

8 cloves garlic, chopped

3 tsps chilli flakes

STAPLES

2 tbsps butter

2 tbsps olive oil

1 tsp salt

Freshly ground pepper

OPTIONAL

¼ cup (10g, ¼ oz) fresh parsley, finely chopped

Heat the butter and oil in a large frying pan over medium heat until the butter begins to foam.

Fry the garlic for 1 minute, then add the chilli and fry for a further minute.

Add the prawns in small batches and fry for 3 minutes or until they are cooked through and orange. Drain them on paper towels.

Season the prawns to taste and serve garnished with parsley.

45 MIN

4

Chorizo and Herb Bread

2 French bread
sticks (about
40cm/15in long)

1 tbsp fresh
oregano, chopped

1 tbsp fresh basil,
chopped

1 tbsp fresh parsley,
chopped

350g (12oz) spicy
chorizo sausages

4 cloves garlic,
crushed

STAPLES

125g (4oz) butter,
room temperature

¼ cup (60ml, 2fl oz)
olive oil

1 tsp salt

OPTIONAL

¼ cup (10g, ¼ oz)
rosemary leaves

Preheat the oven to 180°C (350°F, Gas Mark 4).

Mash the herbs (including rosemary if using) with the butter
until completely mixed through.

Heat half the oil in a frying pan and cook the chorizo for
7 minutes, turning to cook on all sides. Remove from the pan
and let cool for 10 minutes, then cut into 5mm thick slices.

Cut the bread into 1½ cm (¾ in) thick slices, but don't cut
all the way through. Leave about 5mm (¼ in) intact at the
bottom.

Spread small amounts of herb butter on each slice and insert
slices of chorizo in between the slices as well. Brush the tops
with the remaining oil.

Wrap the bread up in foil and bake in the oven for
10 minutes. Then open the tops and bake for a further
5 minutes to crisp up the bread.

Serve hot.

20 MIN

 1 CUP

Aioli

2 cloves garlic, crushed

1 small lemon, juiced

2 tbsps fresh parsley, chopped

½ tsp Dijon mustard

STAPLES

1 large egg yolk

1 cup (250ml, 8fl oz) olive oil

1 tsp salt

Whisk the egg yolk for 1 minute in a large metal bowl with a stick blender until it becomes slightly creamy.

Pour in a small amount of oil and blend thoroughly. Pour in some more ensuring the oil is completely mixed in. Repeat until the mixture thickens and becomes creamy.

Once all the oil is incorporated, whisk in the garlic, lemon juice, parsley, mustard, and salt.

20 MIN
+ CHILLING

4

Ceviche

1kg (2lb) fresh white fish (such as kingfish)

8 large limes, juiced

8 small lemons, juiced

2 red capsicums, finely chopped

2 green chillies, seeded and finely chopped

1 small red onion, finely chopped

STAPLES

Freshly ground salt and pepper

Bring a large pot of water to the boil.

Cook the fish for 1 minute only then remove to a bowl of cold water with ice cubes. Once cooled, drain and pat dry.

Cut the fish into 2cm (1in) cubes and place in a large sealable container with the lime and lemon juice. Mix through and chill for at least 1 hour.

Add the rest of the ingredients, season to taste and serve.

15 MIN

4

Cheese and Ham Quesadilla

8 large flour tortillas

16 slices of ham off the bone (use serrano ham if possible)

1 cup (125g, 4oz) mozzarella cheese, grated

1 cup (125g, 4oz) Colby cheese, grated

1 tsp cayenne pepper

STAPLES

¼ cup (60ml, 2fl oz) olive oil

Freshly ground salt and pepper

OPTIONAL

Oregano leaves, to garnish

Heat a large frying pan over medium heat.

Brush one side of each tortilla with olive oil. Place one tortilla on the pan, oiled side down. Arrange four slices of ham on top and sprinkle over a quarter of the cheeses and a pinch of cayenne and season to taste. Place another tortilla on top, oiled side on the outside.

Fry for 1-2 minutes, until the cheese starts to melt and the bottom tortilla starts to crisp. Carefully flip over and cook for another 2 minutes. Repeat with the other tortillas and fillings. Keep the cooked tortillas somewhere warm in a stack while cooking the others.

To serve, cut each tortilla into wedges and garnish with oregano.

20

PIECES

Croquettes

1½ cups (185g, 6oz) Cheddar cheese, grated

2 large onions, grated and squeezed to remove excess liquid

¼ cup (25g, 1oz) grated Parmesan

4 cups (500g, 1lb 2oz) breadcrumbs

1 pinch nutmeg

STAPLES

3 eggs, lightly whisked

1⅓ cups (165g, 5½ oz) plain flour

2 tbsps butter

1 tbsp olive oil

Vegetable oil, for frying

2 cups (480ml, 1pt) milk

Salt and pepper

Heat the butter and oil in a medium saucepan over medium heat until it begins to foam. Whisk in the onion and ¼ cup of flour and stir for 5 minutes. Add the milk, ¼ cup at a time, whisking to avoid lumps for 8 minutes. Add the cheeses, nutmeg and a couple of grinds of salt and pepper. Stir until boiling, then set aside to cool for 30 minutes. Chill the mixture in the fridge for at least 1 hour (or preferably overnight).

Shape the mixture into 6cm (2½ in) long thick cigars. Place the remaining flour, breadcrumbs and egg in separate shallow dishes. Coat the croquettes in the flour, then the egg, then the breadcrumbs.

Heat 6cm (2½ in) oil in a deep-sided saucepan over high heat. Fry in small batches for 3 minutes until just golden. Drain on paper towels and serve hot.

40 MIN

Patatas Bravas

1 x 400g (14oz) can diced tomatoes, drained

2 spring onions, finely chopped

2 cloves garlic, crushed

1 tsp chilli flakes

1.2kg (2½ lbs) potatoes (use Coliban or Bintje)

¼ cup (10g, ¼ oz) fresh basil, finely shredded

STAPLES

2 tsps red wine vinegar

4 tbsps salt

⅓ cup (80ml, 3fl oz) olive oil

Freshly ground pepper

OPTIONAL

1 tsp smoked paprika

1 tsp ground oregano

Preheat the oven to 200°C (400°F, Gas Mark 6) and line two large baking trays with baking paper.

Place the tomatoes, spring onion, garlic, chilli, vinegar, plus the paprika and oregano if using, in a bowl and combine. Season to taste with salt and pepper and set aside.

Peel the potatoes and cut into wedges. Pat them dry, then sprinkle with half the salt.

Steam the wedges for 10 minutes, then place in a bowl and gently coat with the olive oil and the rest of the salt.

Toast the wedges for 25 minutes until they are browned and crisp.

Serve hot with the tomato salsa and shredded basil on top.

45 MIN

4

Easy Paella

400g (14oz) chorizo sausage, cut into 1cm (½ in) thick slices

1 large red capsicum, seeded and thickly sliced

400g (14oz) prawn tails, shelled and deveined

2 cups (310g, 11oz) medium-grain rice

5 cups (1.25L, 42fl oz) hot chicken stock

¾ cup (175g, 6oz) tomato passata

STAPLES

4 tbsps olive oil

Freshly ground salt and pepper

OPTIONAL

1 cup (170g, 6oz) fresh or frozen peas

Heat 2 tablespoons of the oil in a large, deep-sided frying pan or paella pan over medium heat. Fry the chorizo and capsicum for 6 minutes until the chorizo is just browned. Transfer to a bowl.

Add another 2 tablespoons of oil and fry the prawns for 2 minutes. Add the prawns to the chorizo and capsicum.

Add the rice to the pan and fry for 1 minute, stirring to coat the rice grains in oil. Add ¼ cup of stock and simmer for 4 minutes. Add the passata and stir through until simmering. Then add the rest of the stock. Cover and let it simmer on low heat for 20 minutes or until the rice is just tender.

Stir through the peas, if using, and return the chorizo, capsicum and prawns to the pan and stir through for 5 minutes.

Season to taste and serve with lemon wedges on the side.

Galician Octopus

700g (1½ lb) whole octopus, trimmed (ask your fish monger to do this for you)

4 cups (1L, 2pt) vegetable stock

2 tbsps smoked paprika

500g (1lb) potatoes, peeled and cut into 1cm (½ in) thick slices (Dutch Cream or Kipfler)

STAPLES

4 cups (1L, 2pt) water

¼ cup (60ml, 2fl oz) olive oil

2 tsps salt

Bring the stock and water to a boil in a large pot. Lower the octopus in, tentacles first. Reduce heat and simmer, covered, for 1 hour. Remove the octopus and cut off the tentacles, discarding the rest. Keep the water.

Cut the tentacles into 1cm (½ in) thick slices.

Boil the potatoes in the octopus water for 10 minutes, adding the salt to the water. Once they're tender, drain and arrange in a single layer on the serving plates.

Arrange the sliced octopus over the top of the potato. Drizzle with olive oil and sprinkle the paprika over the top.

Clams with White Wine and Parsley

800g (1¾ lb) fresh clams, rinsed and scrubbed

½ cup (120ml, 4fl oz) white wine

3 large cloves garlic, crushed

2 tsps chilli flakes

½ cup (20g, ¾ oz) fresh parsley, finely chopped

⅔ cup (150ml, 5fl oz) vegetable stock

STAPLES
100g (3½ oz) butter

Heat 1 tablespoon of butter in a large pot over medium heat. Fry the garlic and chilli for 2 minutes then add the rest of the butter. Once it starts to foam, add the clams, turn the heat to medium-high and pour the wine over the top.

Stir until boiling, then add the stock. Simmer for 3 minutes, stirring frequently, until the clams are cooked through.

Serve the clams with some of the liquid and sprinkle over the parsley.

40 MIN

Mediterranean Fish Soup

1 large onion, chopped

3 large cloves garlic, crushed

1 cup (250g, 9oz) cherry tomatoes

1 cup (225g, 8oz) tinned diced tomatoes

2 cups (500ml, 1pt) vegetable stock

800g (1¾ lb) white fish fillets, cut into 2cm (1in) chunks (use whiting or flathead)

STAPLES

2 tbsps olive oil

Freshly ground salt and pepper

OPTIONAL

1 tsp smoked paprika

Fresh thyme, to garnish

Heat the oil in a large saucepan over medium heat. Fry the onion and garlic for 5 minutes. Add the cherry tomatoes, and paprika, if using, and fry for 5 more minutes.

Add the diced tomatoes and stock and bring to a boil. Reduce heat to low and simmer, covered, for 20 minutes.

Add the fish pieces and cook for 5 minutes.

Season to taste and serve garnished with thyme.

30 MIN

Tomato, Beans and Chorizo Soup

300g (10oz) chorizo sausages, chopped

1 tsp smoked paprika

2 cloves garlic, crushed

2 x 400g (14oz) cans diced tomatoes

2 x 400g (14oz) cans kidney beans, drained and rinsed

1⅔ cups (400ml, 13fl oz) chicken stock

STAPLES

½ tbsp olive oil

Freshly ground salt and pepper

OPTIONAL

Fresh basil leaves, to garnish

Heat the oil in a large pot over medium heat. Fry the chorizo, paprika and garlic for 5 minutes until the chorizo starts to brown.

Add the tomatoes, beans and stock and increase the heat to high until it begins to boil.

Reduce heat to low and simmer, covered, for 20 minutes.

Season to taste and serve garnished with fresh basil.

10 MIN
+ SOAKING

Tuna with Beans and Onion Salad

1 large red onion, quartered and finely sliced

600g (1lb 5oz) cooked and flaked tuna (can use tinned tuna)

¼ cup (10g, ¼ oz) fresh parsley, chopped

2 x 400g (14oz) can cannellini beans, drained and rinsed

3 tbsps lemon juice

STAPLES

Salt

Freshly ground pepper

Olive oil

Place the sliced onion in a bowl and rub salt into the slices. Let it sit for 15 minutes. Then cover with warm water and sit for another 15 minutes. Then rinse and drain the onion.

Place the onions, flaked tuna, parsley, beans, juice and a pinch of salt and pepper in a large salad bowl. Drizzle some oil over the top then combine.

Season further to taste then serve.

15 MIN
+ COOLING

Ensaladilla Rusa

800g (1¾ lb) potatoes, peeled and cut into 2cm (1in) cubes (Kipfler or Desiree)

2 carrots, grated

2 cups (340g, 12oz) fresh or frozen peas

1½ cups (365g, 13oz) garlic aioli (shop-bought or see recipe page 220)

2 large gherkins, chopped

1 tsp Dijon mustard

STAPLES

1 tbsp olive oil

Freshly ground salt and pepper

Boil the potatoes in slightly salted water for 10 minutes. Add the peas and cook for 1 more minute. Drain under cold water and let the vegetables cool for 30 minutes.

Place the potato, peas, carrot, aioli, gherkins, mustard and oil in a large salad bowl and mix thoroughly.

Season to taste and serve.

Peri Peri Chicken and Corn

3 cloves garlic,
crushed

4 chicken
Marylands, patted
dry

1 tsp cayenne
pepper (use ½ tsp
for a milder taste)

2 tsps fresh ginger,
minced

3 tbsps sweet
paprika

4 ears corn

STAPLES

2 tbsps olive oil

1 tsp salt

Freshly ground
pepper

2 tbsps butter

OPTIONAL

2 tsps ground
oregano

To make the peri peri sauce, mix the garlic, cayenne, ginger, paprika, oil, salt and a couple of grinds of pepper, and oregano, if using, together in a small bowl.

Coat the chicken in the sauce, cover and marinate for at least 4 hours, preferably overnight.

Steam the corn ears for 15 minutes, then set aside.

Heat a large grill pan over medium-high heat. Grill the chicken for 12 minutes, turning halfway through and basting with leftover marinade. Sit and cover with foil.

Coat the corn with the butter then grill for 2 minutes on each side.

Serve the chicken and corn hot.

55 MIN

Arroz con Pollo

2 x 400g (14oz) cans diced tomatoes

1 onion, chopped

3 cloves garlic, crushed

8 chicken thighs, skin on, bone in

80g (3oz) smoked ham, chopped

1½ cups (235g, 7oz) long-grain rice

STAPLES

3 tbsps olive oil

1 tsp sugar

2 cups (500ml, 1pt) water (or use chicken stock)

Freshly ground salt and pepper

OPTIONAL

½ tbsp ground oregano

1 cup (140g, 5oz) green olives, pitted

1 lime, sliced

Place ½ cup of the tomatoes in a blender or use a stick blender to puree them to a smooth paste. Set aside.

Heat the oil over medium heat in a large, deep-sided pan. Add the onion and garlic (and oregano, if using) and fry for 5 minutes. Fry the chicken pieces in batches for 10 minutes until browned on each side. Remove from the pan. Add the ham and fry for 2 minutes. Stir in the pureed tomatoes and cook for another 2 minutes.

Add the rice and cook for 1 minute, stirring to coat the grains. Add the rest of the tomatoes and the sugar, stir through and add the water (or stock) and bring to a boil. Reduce heat to low and add the chicken. Cover and cook for 20 minutes, then stir through the olives if using.

Season to taste and serve with the chicken arranged over the rice and garnished with slices of lime.

50 MIN

Tomato and Squash Tortilla

4 yellow squash, cut into 5mm (¼ in) thick rounds

12 cherry tomatoes, halved

1 small red capsicum, seeded, halved and sliced

1 onion, chopped

1 cup (125g, 4oz) cheese, grated (Swiss or Edam)

8 large eggs, lightly beaten

STAPLES

1 tbsp olive oil

¼ cup (50ml, 2fl oz) milk

Freshly ground salt and pepper

Preheat oven to 220°C (425°F, Gas Mark 7).

Heat the oil in a large oven-proof frying pan over medium heat. Fry the onion for 5 minutes until softened. Add the squash, tomatoes and capsicum and cook for 5 more minutes, covered. Remove the pan from the heat.

Whisk the eggs together with the cheese, milk and a couple of grinds of salt and pepper. Pour over the vegetables in the pan, gently lifting up the vegetables to let the egg coat the bottom of the pan. Heat on medium-low until the sides only are cooked.

Place the pan in the oven and bake for 15 minutes or until the egg is set in the middle.

To serve, slide a spatula around the edges and carefully turn out upside down onto a large serving dish.

50 MIN

Spanish Omelette

1 onion, quartered and sliced

600g (1lb 5oz) potatoes, peeled, halved and cut into 5mm (¼ in) slices (Desiree or Nicola)

2 cloves garlic, crushed

½ tbsp lemon juice

1 cup (30g, 1oz) baby spinach, roughly chopped

6 eggs, lightly beaten

STAPLES

½ cup (125ml, 4fl oz) olive oil

Freshly ground salt and pepper

Heat the oil in a large deep-sided frying pan over medium-high heat. Fry the onion and garlic for 2 minutes. Add the potatoes with a couple of grinds of salt and pepper and fry for about 20 minutes until the potatoes are just tender. Remove from the pan and reserve 1 tablespoon of the oil.

Heat the reserved oil in a large non-stick frying pan over medium heat and add the eggs, spinach and potato mixture. Gently stir for 5 minutes until it starts to set. Stop stirring and cook for 4 more minutes. Carefully cover the pan with a large plate, invert the tortilla onto the plate, then return the tortilla to the pan with the cooked side on top.

Cook for another 5 minutes until the egg is completely set. Remove from the pan and serve warm.

45 MIN

Mediterranean Prawn Stew

350g (12oz) prawn tails, shelled and deveined

4 large cloves garlic, crushed

2 small zucchini, quartered lengthways and sliced

1 large onion, chopped

1 x 400g (14oz) can diced tomatoes

¼ cup (60ml, 2fl oz) orange juice

STAPLES

2 tbsps olive oil

Freshly ground salt and pepper

2 cups (500ml, 1pt) water (or use vegetable stock)

OPTIONAL

1 small yellow capsicum, seeded and cubed

¼ cup (10g, ¼ oz) fresh parsley, chopped

Heat the oil in a large pot over medium heat. Fry the onion and garlic for 5 minutes.

Add the zucchini (and capsicum, if using) and fry for 2 minutes. Add the tomatoes, water (or stock) and half the parsley, if using, and bring to a boil. Reduce heat to low and simmer, uncovered, for 25 minutes.

Add the prawns and orange juice and simmer for 5 minutes or until the prawns are cooked.

Season to taste and serve garnished with the rest of the parsley.

1 HR, 30 MIN

Empanadas

1 large onion, finely chopped

3 cloves garlic, crushed

500g (1lb) lean minced beef

1½ tsps ground cumin

2 small tomatoes, seeds removed, finely chopped

1kg (2lb) shortcrust pastry

STAPLES

2 tbsps olive oil

1 egg, lightly beaten

Freshly ground salt and pepper

Vegetable oil, for frying

OPTIONAL

1 green chilli, deseeded and finely chopped

1 tsp smoked paprika

Heat the olive oil in a large frying pan over medium-high heat. Add the onion and fry for 5 minutes until softened and browned. Add the garlic and fry for a further 1 minute. Add the beef and cumin (and chilli and paprika, if using) and fry for 8 minutes, until the beef is cooked and browned. Add the tomatoes and stir through. Cook for a further 2 minutes. Season with salt and pepper then set aside to cool.

To assemble the empanadas, roll out the pastry to about 3mm (⅛ in) thick and cut into roughly 9cm (3½ in) circles. Keep reusing and rolling out the pastry until it is all used up.

Place 1 dessertspoon of filling on one half of each circle, leaving a 1cm (½ in) edge clear.

Brush the edges with egg. Roll over the other half of the pastry and try to remove any air pockets before sealing. Use a fork to press down on the edges to seal.

Heat about 2cm (1in) of vegetable oil in a large deep-sided frying pan.

Fry the empanadas in batches for 12 minutes, turning halfway, until crisp and golden on both sides.

Serve hot.

Beef and Bean Stew

1 large onion, chopped

1 x 400g (14oz) cans four-bean mix, drained and rinsed

600g (1lb 5oz) stewing steak, cut into thin slices

3 cups (400g, 14oz) pumpkin, cut into 1½ cm (¾ in) chunks

2 x 400g (14oz) cans diced tomatoes

2 cups (500ml, 1pt) beef stock

STAPLES

2 tbsps olive oil

2 cups (500ml, 1pt) water

Freshly ground salt and pepper

OPTIONAL

3 cloves garlic, crushed

1 tsp smoked paprika

Heat the oil in a large saucepan over medium-high heat. Add the onion and fry for 5 minutes until softened and browned. Add the garlic, if using, and fry for a further minute. Add the beef and fry in batches for 5 minutes until browned then return all the beef to the pot.

Add the pumpkin, beans, tomatoes, stock, water, half the thyme, as well as the paprika if using, and bring to a boil. Reduce to a simmer and cook, covered, for 1 ½ hours until the beef is tender.

Stir in the olives, if using, and simmer for another 15 minutes.

Season to taste and serve garnished with remaining thyme.

2 HR

Cuban Picadillo

2 onions, chopped

1kg (2lb) minced beef

2 tbsps mixed dried herbs

1 x 400g (14oz) can diced tomatoes, drained

1 cup (160g, 6oz) raisins

¼ cup (35g, 1¼ oz) capers, drained

STAPLES

2 tbsps olive oil

1⅔ cups (400ml, 13fl oz) water (or use beef stock)

Freshly ground salt and pepper

OPTIONAL

1 tsp allspice

⅔ cup (95g, 3oz) green olives, pitted and chopped

Heat the oil in a large frying pan over medium heat. Fry the onions for 5 minutes until softened. Increase the heat to medium-high and add the beef and herbs (and allspice, if using) and fry for 8 minutes until the beef is browned.

Add the tomatoes and water (or stock) and bring to a boil. Reduce heat to low and simmer, covered, for 1 hour.

Add the raisins and capers and cook, uncovered, for 20 minutes more.

Stir through the olives, if using, and season to taste.

45 MIN

4

Chorizo, Chickpea and Kale Stew

2 onions, chopped

2 tsps smoked paprika

600g (1lb 5oz) chorizo sausages, cut into 5mm (¼ in) thick slices

2 cups (500ml, 1pt) passata

1 x 400g (14oz) can chickpeas

3 cups (400g, 14oz) kale, roughly chopped

STAPLES

2 tbsps olive oil

2 cups (500ml, 1pt) water (or use chicken stock)

Freshly ground salt and pepper

OPTIONAL

3 cloves garlic, crushed

Heat the oil in a large saucepan over medium heat. Fry the onions for 5 minutes until softened. Increase the heat to medium-high and add the paprika and chorizo. Fry for 5 minutes until the chorizo is browned. Add the garlic, if using, and fry for a further 1 minute.

Add the passata, chickpeas and water and bring to a boil. Reduce to low and simmer, covered, for 30 minutes.

Stir through the kale and simmer for another 10 minutes.

Season to taste and serve.

1 HR, 30 MIN

Chicken and Tomato Stew

8 chicken drumsticks

1 large green capsicum, seeded and chopped

1 cup (250g, 9oz) cherry tomatoes, halved

1 large onion, chopped

3 cloves garlic, crushed

1 cup (225g, 8oz) tomato passata

STAPLES

2 tbsps olive oil

1¼ cups (300ml, 10fl oz) water (or use chicken stock)

1 tsp sugar

Freshly ground salt and pepper

OPTIONAL

1 tbsp dried mixed herbs

Preheat oven to 180°C (350°F, Gas Mark 4).

Heat the oil in a large heatproof casserole dish over medium heat. Fry the onion and garlic for 5 minutes until softened. Add the chicken in batches and cook for 5 minutes until the skin is lightly browned and remove from the dish.

Add ¼ cup passata along with the capsicum and tomatoes. Cook for 5 more minutes. Add the rest of the passata, the water (or stock), mixed herbs, if using, and sugar. Bring to a boil.

Place in the oven and bake, covered, for 1 hour.

Season to taste and serve.

1 HR

4

Spanish Rice

1 onion, finely
chopped

2 cloves garlic,
crushed

1 cup (155g, 4oz)
long-grain rice

1 tbsp tomato paste

1 x 400g (14oz) can
chopped tomatoes

2 cups (500ml, 1pt)
chicken stock

STAPLES

⅓ cup (75ml, 2½
fl oz) olive oil

½ tsp sugar

Freshly ground salt
and pepper

OPTIONAL

2 tbsps jalapenos,
finely chopped

Preheat oven to 180°C (350°F, Gas Mark 4).

Heat the oil in a large heatproof casserole
dish over medium heat. Fry the onions
and garlic for 5 minutes until softened.
Add the jalapenos, if using, and cook for a
further 1 minute.

Stir through the rice for 4 minutes then turn
the heat down to low.

Stir through the tomato paste for 1 minute
then add the tomatoes, stock and sugar and
bring to a simmer.

Place the dish in the oven, covered, and cook
for 25 minutes or until the rice is tender.

Let it sit for 10 minutes, covered, then
season to taste and serve.

1 HR, 20 MIN

 4

Ratatouille

2 large zucchinis, cut into quarters lengthways and thickly sliced

1 large onion, chopped

1 large eggplant, cut into 1½ cm (¾ in) cubes

1 x 400g (14oz) can diced tomatoes

2 tbsps rosemary, chopped

1 cup (250ml, 8fl oz) hot vegetable stock

STAPLES

1½ tbsps olive oil

1 cup (250ml, 8fl oz) water

½ tsp sugar

Freshly ground salt and pepper

OPTIONAL

4 cloves garlic, crushed

Heat the oil in a large saucepan over medium heat. Fry the onions (and garlic, if using) for 5 minutes until softened. Increase the heat to medium-high and add the eggplant and fry for 5 minutes.

Add the tomatoes, half the rosemary, the stock, water and sugar and bring to a boil. Reduce the heat to low and simmer, covered, for 40 minutes.

Stir in the zucchini and simmer for 15 minutes or until the zucchini is tender.

Season to taste and serve garnished with the remaining rosemary.

50 MIN

Spanish Chorizo Meatballs

250g (9oz) chorizo
sausage, finely
minced

600g (1lb 5oz)
minced beef

½ cup (60g, 2oz)
breadcrumbs

2 small red
onions, grated and
squeezed to remove
excess liquid

1 tsp chilli flakes

¼ cup (10g, ¼ oz)
basil, chopped, plus
extra leaves, to
garnish

STAPLES

1½ tbsps olive oil

Freshly ground salt
and pepper

OPTIONAL

½ tbsp smoked
paprika

Heat 1 tablespoon oil in a frying pan over medium-high heat.
Fry the onions for 4 minutes, then stir through the chilli (and
paprika, if using) for 1 minute.

Remove the onions to a large mixing bowl with the
chorizo, mince, breadcrumbs and a couple of grinds of salt
and pepper.

Form the mixture into balls approximately 3cm (1in) wide.

Heat the rest of the olive oil in the pan. Fry the meatballs
in small batches for 12 minutes, turning frequently to cook
all over.

Serve hot, garnished with fresh basil leaves.

1 HR, 30 MIN

Chicken Patatas Bravas

500g (1lb) chicken thigh fillets, cut into bite-size chunks

500g (1lb) potatoes, peeled and cut into 3cm (1in) chunks

1 tbsp fresh thyme, chopped

1 cup (245g, 9oz) aioli (see recipe page 220)

4 cloves garlic, crushed

8 cherry tomatoes, chopped

STAPLES

⅓ cup (80ml, 3fl oz) olive oil

¼ cup (60ml, 2fl oz) water

Freshly ground salt and pepper

OPTIONAL

1 tbsp dried mixed herbs

Preheat the oven to 190°C (375°F, Gas Mark 5).

Heat 1 tablespoon olive oil in a large frying pan over medium-high heat. Add the chicken and garlic and fry in 2 batches for 6 minutes until the chicken is browned, then remove the chicken from the pan.

Add 2 tablespoons oil to the pan and fry the potatoes in batches for 5 minutes, stirring to coat in the oil.

Place the potatoes, chicken, any juices from the pan, the thyme, tomatoes, mixed herbs, if using, and the rest of the oil in a casserole dish. Stir everything around to combine. Pour over the water, cover and bake for 30 minutes. Remove the lid and roast for another 15 minutes until the potatoes are softened and browned.

Season to taste and serve hot drizzled with aioli.

1 HR
+ CHILLING

Spanish Flan

1 tbsp orange zest

6 large fresh eggs, beaten

2 cups (500ml, 1pt) condensed milk

STAPLES

1 tsp vanilla extract

2 cups (500ml, 1pt) milk

¾ cup (165g, 6oz) caster sugar

¼ cup (60ml, 2fl oz) water

Preheat the oven to 175°C (350°F, Gas Mark 4) and lightly oil six dessert ramekins (1¼ cup capacity) and place them in a large deep-sided baking dish.

Vigorously whisk together the eggs, condensed milk, vanilla, milk and zest.

Divide the flan mixture between the ramekins and place in the lower third of the oven. Fill the baking dish with enough water to come halfway up the sides of the flans.

Bake for 40 minutes, ensuring there is always water in the dish. The flans are cooked when a skewer inserted into the middle comes out clean.

Sit the flans for at least 4 hours in the refrigerator then turn them out upside down onto serving plates.

Heat the sugar and water in a saucepan over medium-high heat until the sugar is dissolved and the liquid turns golden brown. Immediately pour over the flans and serve.

Churros

1 tsp cinnamon plus 2 tsps for dusting

STAPLES

3 cups (375g, 12oz) plain flour

1 tsp baking powder

1 tsp salt

2½ cups (600ml, 21fl oz) water

2 tbsps caster sugar plus ½ cup (110g, 4oz) for dusting

2 egg yolks

Vegetable oil for frying

Sift the cinnamon, flour, baking powder and salt into a large mixing bowl.

Boil the water in a small saucepan. Reduce to a simmer, add the sugar and stir until dissolved. Pour into the flour mix. Whisk until the mixture is fluffy and smooth. Add the egg yolks one at a time and keep whisking until the batter is shiny, then pour into a pastry piping bag.

Heat a large saucepan with 5cm (2in) vegetable oil over high heat. Pipe 10cm (4in) lengths of batter into the oil, using a knife to cut off the lengths. Fry for 3-4 minutes until golden brown. Drain on paper towels.

Mix together the cinnamon and caster sugar for dusting in a shallow dish. Dredge the churros in the sugar and serve hot.

NOTE: You need a dedicated cloth or heavy-duty plastic piping bag to make these. A disposable plastic bag isn't strong enough.

45 MIN

Baked Rice Pudding

1 tsp finely grated lemon zest

½ tsp cinnamon

¾ cup (130g, 4oz) short-grain rice (such as Arborio)

⅓ cup (100ml, 3½ fl oz) thickened cream

STAPLES

40g (1½ oz) unsalted butter, room temperature

1 tsp vanilla extract

3½ cups (900ml, 30fl oz) milk

½ cup (105g, 4oz) caster sugar

Preheat oven to 175°C (350°F, Gas Mark 4) and lightly butter a 20 x 10cm (8 x 4in) baking dish.

Place the zest, cinnamon, rice, vanilla, milk and cream in a large saucepan and bring to a boil, stirring frequently to ensure nothing sticks to the bottom.

Reduce the heat to low, stir in the sugar and simmer for 10 minutes, stirring to dissolve the sugar.

Pour the mixture into the baking dish and bake, covered, for 20 minutes. Remove the cover and bake for a further 10 minutes until the top has browned and the rice is tender.

Serve warm.

10 MIN

Sangria

5 oranges;
1 quartered and
sliced, 4 juiced
to make 1¼ cups
(300ml, 10fl oz)

2 small limes,
quartered and
sliced

1 large nashi pear,
cored, quartered
and sliced

¾ cup (200ml, 7fl
oz) brandy

4½ cups (1.25L,
38fl oz) dry red wine

2 cups (500ml, 1pt)
soda water

STAPLES

¼ cup (55g, 2oz)
caster sugar

Pour the orange juice, brandy, red wine,
soda water and sugar into a large pouring
jug and stir to dissolve the sugar.

Add the fruit and some ice cubes and serve.

moroccan

1 HR

1

CUP

Harissa

3 cloves garlic,
crushed

2 tbsps cumin
seeds

3 tbsps coriander
seeds

1 bird's-eye chilli,
seeds removed,
chopped

1 tbsp sweet
paprika

2 small red
capsicums

STAPLES

3 tbsps olive oil

½ tsp salt

Freshly ground
pepper

OPTIONAL

1 tsp fennel seeds

Preheat the oven to 200°C (400°F, Gas
Mark 6)

Lightly coat the capsicums with oil and
place on a baking tray. Roast for 35 minutes,
turning every 10 minutes, or until the skin
is charred and blackened in most places.
Place them in a covered container and let
them sweat for 10 minutes. Peel off the skin,
remove the seeds and roughly chop the flesh.

Heat a frying pan over medium-high heat
and dry fry the cumin and coriander (and
fennel seeds, if using) for about 2 minutes,
stirring constantly until they begin to brown.
Place them in a mortar and pestle and grind
them to powder.

Place all the ingredients in a blender or food
processor and puree until almost smooth.
Season to taste and serve.

40 MIN

Moroccan Flatbreads

1 portion flatbread dough (see recipe page 173)

1 clove garlic, crushed

½ tbsp ground oregano

¼ cup (40g, 1½ oz) black sesame seeds

250g (9oz) feta, crumbled

1 pinch turmeric

STAPLES

⅓ cup (100ml, 3½ fl oz) olive oil

Preheat the oven to 190°C (375°F, Gas Mark 5). Lightly oil two large baking trays.

Divide the dough mixture into 6 pieces and roll out into roughly 16cm (6in) circles.

Whisk together the oil, garlic, oregano and turmeric and brush the tops of the dough with the mixture. Bake for 15 minutes, then remove from the oven.

Sprinkle the feta over the top of the breads and the sesame seeds over that.

Bake for 10 minutes, or until the dough is browned on the edges and the cheese has melted.

Serve warm.

3 HR

Lamb, Pumpkin and Apricot Tagine

1 large onion, roughly chopped

1 tbsp ras el hanout (see recipe page 272)

600g (1lb 5oz) lamb necks, cut into 2½cm (2in) chunks

8 Roma tomatoes, chopped

1 small butternut pumpkin, cut into 3cm (1in) chunks

1½ cups (300g, 10oz) dried apricots

STAPLES

2 tbsps olive oil

2 cups (500ml, 1pt) water (or use vegetable stock)

Freshly ground salt and pepper

OPTIONAL

1 stick cinnamon

1 tsp ground cumin

Fresh coriander leaves, to garnish

Heat the oil in a large heatproof tagine (or heatproof casserole dish) over medium heat. Fry the onion for 6 minutes. Add the ras el hanout, plus the cinnamon stick and cumin if using, and fry for another minute. Add the lamb and fry for 5 minutes until slightly browned.

Stir through the tomatoes, pumpkin, apricots and water (or stock). Stir to mix then bring to a boil. Reduce heat to low and simmer, covered, for 2 hours, adding more water as needed. Stir every 30 minutes.

Remove the lid and cook for another 30 minutes until the mixture is nearly dry.

Season to taste, garnish with coriander leaves and serve.

1 HR, 20 MIN

Chicken Apricot Tagine

3 cloves garlic, crushed

1kg (2lb) assorted chicken pieces

4 cups (540g, 1¼ lb) butternut pumpkin, cut into 3cm (1in) chunks

2 cups (380g, 13oz) dried apricots

2 tbsps agave syrup

Seeds from 2 pomegranates

STAPLES

2 tbsps olive oil

1⅓ cups (350ml, (12fl oz) water (or use chicken stock)

Freshly ground salt and pepper

OPTIONAL

1 tbsp lemon juice

Fresh mint leaves, to garnish

Heat the oil in a large heatproof tagine (or heatproof casserole dish) over medium heat. Fry the garlic for 2 minutes. Add the chicken pieces and fry for 6 minutes in batches until they're slightly browned.

Stir through the pumpkin, apricots, water (or stock), syrup and lemon juice, if using. Stir to mix then bring to a boil. Reduce heat to low and simmer, covered, for 30 minutes.

Remove the lid and cook for another 20 minutes until the mixture is nearly dry.

Season to taste, garnish with pomegranate seeds and mint leaves and serve.

1 HR, 15 MIN

Cabbage and Sausage Tagine

2 small onions, chopped

750g (1½ lb) smoked pork sausage, cut into 5mm (¼ in) slices

2 cups (270g, 9oz) butternut pumpkin, cut into 2cm (1in) chunks

1 small carrot, finely chopped

1 medium head white cabbage, stalk removed, roughly chopped

1 cup (250ml, 8fl oz) vegetable stock

STAPLES

2 tbsps butter

1 tbsp olive oil

Freshly ground salt and pepper

OPTIONAL

½ cup (20g, ¾ oz) fresh parsley, finely chopped

Heat the butter and oil in a large heatproof tagine (or heatproof casserole dish) over medium heat. Fry the onion for 6 minutes. Add the sausage and fry for 3 minutes.

Add the pumpkin and carrot and cook for 4 more minutes. Add the cabbage in batches, adding more once the previous batch has reduced in size. Add the stock. Stir to mix then bring to a boil. Reduce heat to low and simmer, covered, for 30 minutes.

Remove the lid, stir through the parsley if using and cook for another 20 minutes.

Season to taste and serve.

4

Sausage with Vegetables and Chickpeas

8 Calabrese (or Continental-style) pork sausages

3 red capsicums, seeded and cut into large chunks

3 yellow capsicums, seeded and cut into large chunks

1 x 400g (14oz) can chickpeas, drained and rinsed

4 small squash, cut into chunks

3 cloves garlic, crushed

STAPLES

3 tbsps olive oil

Freshly ground salt and pepper

OPTIONAL

3 tsps lemon juice

Cooked couscous, to serve

Toss the vegetables and chickpeas with the garlic, 2 tbsps of oil, lemon juice (if using) and a couple of grinds of salt and pepper.

Place the sausages in a heatproof bowl and just cover with boiling water. Let them sit for 10 minutes, then remove and pat dry.

Heat 1 tablespoon of oil in a frying pan over medium-high heat. Fry the sausages for 10 minutes or until cooked through. Remove and set aside. Fry the chickpeas over low heat for 5 minutes. Add the vegetables and cook for a further 15 minutes with the lid on until they're tender, stirring frequently. Remove everything from the pan and place in a sealed container to sweat for 5 minutes before serving.

Serve with a side of couscous.

10 MIN

1 CUP

Basic Ras el Hanout

3 tsps ground ginger

3 tsps ground cardamom

1½ tsps ground coriander seeds

3 tsps ground mace

1½ tsps turmeric

1½ tsps ground anise seeds

STAPLES

1 tsp ground black pepper

1 tsp ground white pepper

OPTIONAL

1½ tsps ground cinnamon

1½ tsps ground allspice

1 tsp ground nutmeg

1 tsp cayenne

½ tsp ground cloves

Combine all the spices together and stir to mix thoroughly.

Store in a sealed container; will keep for a few months.

NOTE: Use the pictured ingredients for a basic and workable version of this spice mix or add the optional extras for a greater depth of flavour.

1 HR

Shakshuka

2 medium onions, quartered and thickly sliced

3 small cloves garlic, crushed

4 red capsicums, chopped

2 x 400g (14oz) cans diced tomatoes

1 tbsp ras el hanout (see recipe page 272)

1 tbsp lemon juice

STAPLES

3 tbsps olive oil

½ tsp sugar

1 cup (250ml, 8fl oz) water (or use vegetable stock)

Freshly ground salt and pepper

4 large eggs, room temperature

Heat the oil in a large heavy-based frying pan over medium heat. Fry the onions for 8 minutes until softened and translucent. Add the garlic, capsicum and ras el hanout and cook for 4 minutes.

Add in the tomatoes, lemon juice, sugar and water (or stock), stir to combine and bring to a boil.

Reduce to a simmer, cover and cook for 20 minutes, stirring occasionally. Season to taste.

Make four wells in the mixture and crack an egg into each. Cook for 5 minutes over low heat, uncovered, then a further 2 minutes covered until the eggs are set to how you like them. Serve hot.

**1 HR, 20 MIN
+ CHILLING**

Moroccan Couscous Soup

700g (1½ lb)
minced lamb

¾ cup (200g, 7oz)
harissa paste
(shop-bought or see
recipe page 264)

2 large onions;
1 grated and
squeezed to remove
excess liquid,
1 chopped

1 tbsp ras el hanout
(shop-bought or see
recipe page 272)

1 x 400g (14oz) can
diced tomatoes

1 cup (170g, 6oz)
pearl couscous

STAPLES

Freshly ground salt
and pepper

4 tbsps olive oil

1 tsp sugar

5 cups (1.25L,
42fl oz) water
(or use 4 cups
vegetable stock
and 1 cup water)

OPTIONAL

3 cloves garlic,
crushed

Mix together the lamb, ½ cup harissa, grated onion, half the
ras el hanout, half the garlic, if using, and a couple of grinds
of salt and pepper. Form into 2½ cm (1in) wide meatballs then
place in the refrigerator for at least 1 hour.

Heat 1 tablespoon of oil in a large frying pan over medium-
high heat. Cook the meatballs in batches for 8 minutes,
turning frequently to cook all over. Remove the meatballs
from the pan and set aside.

Heat the rest of the oil in a large pot over medium heat. Fry
the chopped onion for 5 minutes, then add the rest of the
harissa, ras el hanout and the garlic, if using, and fry for 5
more minutes.

Add the tomatoes, sugar and ½ cup of the water (or stock)
and the meatballs. Bring to a boil, then reduce the heat and
simmer for 10 minutes.

Pour in the rest of the water and the couscous and stir
through gently. Bring to a simmer and cook, covered, for
10 minutes, stirring occasionally, until the couscous is tender.

Remove from the heat, season to taste and serve hot.

**1 HR, 15 MIN
+ CHILLING**

Chicken Kofte Tagine

¼ cup (10g, ¼ oz) parsley, finely chopped

1kg (2lb) chicken mince

1 large onion, finely chopped

16 baby vine tomatoes, half chopped

2 small yellow capsicums, deseeded, halved and sliced

1¼ cups (300ml, 10fl oz) chicken stock

STAPLES

3 tbsps olive oil

Freshly ground salt and pepper

OPTIONAL

3 cloves garlic, crushed

1 tbsp ras el hanout (shop-bought or see recipe page 272)

Add half the parsley, and the ras el hanout, if using, to the chicken mince and stir through. Form the mixture into 2½ cm (1in) wide meatballs then place in the refrigerator for at least 1 hour.

Heat 2 tablespoons of oil in a large frying pan over medium-high heat. Cook the meatballs in batches for 8 minutes, turning frequently to cook all over. Remove the meatballs from the pan and set aside.

Heat the rest of oil in a large heatproof tagine (or heatproof casserole dish) over medium heat. Fry the onion and garlic, if using, for 6 minutes. Add the chopped tomatoes and capsicum and fry for 3 minutes to heat through.

Add the stock, whole tomatoes and meatballs to the tagine and bring to a boil. Reduce heat to low and simmer, covered, for 30 minutes.

Season to taste and serve.

4 HR, 20 MIN

Braised Pork

1kg (2lb) pork shoulder, bone removed

8 shallots, finely chopped

2 tsps fennel seeds

2 large oranges; 1 juiced and zested, 1 cut into wedges

1¼ cups (300ml, 10fl oz) chicken stock

⅔ cup (150ml, 5fl oz) brandy

STAPLES

2 tbsps olive oil

1½ tsps salt

1 tsp ground pepper

OPTIONAL

4 cloves garlic, crushed

Preheat oven to 160°C (350°F, Gas Mark 3).

Cut the shoulder up into about six large chunks and rub the fennel seeds, salt and pepper into them.

Heat the oil in a heatproof casserole dish over medium heat. Fry the shallots (and garlic, if using) for 6 minutes. Add the pork and fry in batches for 5 minutes. Remove pork and add 1 tablespoon orange zest, ¼ cup orange juice and the brandy and bring to a boil, scraping off any bits from the bottom.

Return the meat to the pan and pour over ¾ cup of stock. Roast the pork in the oven, covered, for 4 hours, adding more stock as needed to keep it moist.

Season to taste with salt and pepper and serve garnished with orange slices.

25 MIN

Jewelled Rice

1½ cups (235g, 7oz) long-grain rice, drained and rinsed

¼ tsp turmeric

2¼ cups (560ml, 19 fl oz) vegetable stock

¾ cup (120g, 4oz) currants

Seeds from 1 large pomegranate

⅔ cup (85g, 3oz) toasted pistachios

STAPLES

50g (2oz) butter

2 tbsps olive oil

Freshly ground salt and pepper

OPTIONAL

1 tsp ground oregano

Heat the butter and oil in a large, deep-sided frying pan over medium heat. Add the rice and turmeric (and oregano, if using) and fry for 2 minutes, ensuring the rice is coated.

Add the stock and currants and a couple of grinds of salt and pepper. Bring to a boil, then reduce heat to a simmer. Cover and cook for 15 minutes until the rice is just cooked. Let it stand for another 5 minutes, covered.

Stir in the pomegranate seeds and pistachios. Season further to taste and garnish with parsley.

Lemon Chicken Stew

3 chicken breasts, skinless, cut into 2cm (1in) chunks

1½ cups (340g, 12oz) pearl couscous

2 medium lemons; 1 zested and juiced, 1 cut into wedges

1 x 400g (14oz) can diced tomatoes

⅔ cup (95g, 3oz) black olives, pitted and sliced

1⅔ cups (400ml, 13fl oz) chicken stock

STAPLES

50g (2oz) butter

2 tbsps olive oil

Freshly ground salt and pepper

OPTIONAL

3 cloves garlic, crushed

1 tsp ground oregano

Fresh parsley leaves, to garnish

Heat the butter and oil in a large deep-sided frying pan over medium heat. Fry the garlic and oregano, if using, for 1 minute. Add the chicken in batches and cook for 8 minutes until just browned. Return all the chicken to the pan with the couscous and cook for 5 minutes to coat the couscous.

Add ½ tablespoon lemon zest, 2 tablespoons lemon juice, the tomatoes and stock. Bring to a boil, then reduce to low and simmer, covered, for 15 minutes.

Once the couscous is tender, stir through the olives, season to taste and serve hot, garnished with parsley.

**50 MIN
+ MARINATING**

Harissa Chicken with Olives, Tomato and Garlic

4 x 200g (7oz) chicken breast fillets, halved lengthways

⅓ cup (90g, 3oz) harissa paste (shop-bought or see recipe page 264)

2 cups (500g, 1lb) cherry tomatoes

2 small heads garlic, cut in half across the cloves

1½ cups (210g, 8oz) black olives, pitted

1 small lemon

STAPLES

3 tbsps olive oil

Freshly ground salt and pepper

Preheat the oven to 190°C (380°F, Gas Mark 4) and line a large baking tray with baking paper.

Coat the chicken pieces with the harissa paste and set aside for 30 minutes.

Scatter the tomatoes and garlic heads over the baking tray and drizzle with half the oil. Roast for 20 minutes then add the fillets and olives and drizzle those with the rest of the oil and a squeeze or two of lemon juice.

Roast for 20 minutes or until the chicken is cooked through.

1 HR

1
CUP

Paprika Dip

2 small red
capsicums

3 large cloves
garlic, skin on

150g (5oz) feta

½ cup (60g, 2oz)
toasted walnuts,
roughly chopped

1 tsp sweet paprika

½ tsp cayenne
pepper

STAPLES

2 tbsps olive oil

Freshly ground salt
and pepper

Preheat the oven to 200°C (400°F, Gas
Mark 6).

Lightly brush the capsicums with olive oil
and bake for 40 minutes, turning frequently,
until the skins are mostly blistered and
charred. Add the garlic cloves for the last
15 minutes. Place them in a sealed container
for 15 minutes to sweat and cool down.

Peel off the capsicum skins, remove the
seeds and roughly chop the flesh.

Place the decanted garlic cloves, capsicum,
feta, walnuts, paprika, cayenne and half the
oil in a blender and pulse until you have a
thick, granular dip.

Season to taste with salt and pepper and
serve with oil drizzled over the top.

2 HR, 45 MIN

Spiced Lamb and Sweet Potato Stew

1 medium onion, finely chopped

4 cloves garlic, crushed

1kg (2lb) lamb neck or leg, cut into 3cm (1in) chunks

1 x 400g (14oz) can diced tomatoes

2 medium sweet potatoes, peeled and cut into 2cm (1in) cubes

1 large lemon, zested and juiced

STAPLES

3 tbsps olive oil

3 cups (800ml, 27 fl oz) water (or use vegetable stock)

Freshly ground salt and pepper

OPTIONAL

1 carrot, chopped

½ cup (60g, 2oz) flaked almonds

Fresh parsley, chopped, to garnish

Heat the oil in a large heatproof casserole dish over medium heat. Fry the onion for 5 minutes then add the garlic and cook for another 1 minute.

Fry the lamb in batches for 4 minutes to brown and remove. Pour in ½ cup water (or stock) and scrape up any bits from the bottom. Add the tomatoes, sweet potatoes and carrot, if using, and cook for 10 minutes.

Return the lamb to the pan with the rest of the water, 2 teaspoons lemon zest and 1 tablespoon lemon juice. Bring to a boil, then reduce to a simmer and cook, covered, for 2 hours. Add more liquid if needed.

Season and stir through the almonds, if using. Serve garnished with lemon zest and parsley.

45 MIN

Moroccan-Style Lentils and Chickpeas

1 onion, chopped

½ tbsp harissa paste (see recipe page 264)

1 x 400g (14oz) can diced tomatoes

⅔ cup (120g, 4oz) green lentils, rinsed

2 x 400g (14oz) cans chickpeas, drained and rinsed

1 cup (250ml, 8fl oz) Greek yoghurt, room temperature

STAPLES

3 tbsps olive oil

2½ cups (600ml, 21fl oz) water (or use chicken stock)

Freshly ground salt and pepper

OPTIONAL

½ tbsp ras el hanout (shop-bought or see recipe page 272)

3 cups (400g, 14oz) tightly packed kale, stems removed, roughly chopped

Fresh coriander leaves, to garnish

Heat the oil in a large, heavy-based frying pan over medium heat. Fry the onions for 5 minutes. Add the harissa paste, ras el hanout, if using, ½ teaspoon salt and some pepper and fry for 1 minute.

Add the tomatoes and water (or stock) and bring to a boil. Stir through the lentils and chickpeas, reduce to low heat and simmer, covered, for 25 minutes until the lentils are cooked through.

Stir in the kale, if using, and the yoghurt and cook for 5 more minutes, uncovered. Season to taste and serve garnished with coriander leaves.

**40 MIN
+ CHILLING**

Moroccan Meatballs

800g (1¾ lb) minced lamb

2 cups (60g, 2oz) tightly packed baby spinach leaves, finely chopped

3 cloves garlic, crushed

2 onions, grated and squeezed to remove excess liquid

3 tbsps preserved lemon, finely chopped

1½ tbsps garam masala

STAPLES

3 tbsps olive oil

Freshly ground salt and pepper

OPTIONAL

Fresh parsley leaves, to garnish

1 lemon, cut into wedges, to garnish

Place the lamb, spinach, garlic, onion, preserved lemon, garam masala and a couple of grinds of salt and pepper in a large bowl and mix together thoroughly.

Mould the mix into meatballs around 2½ cm (1in) across. Place in the refrigerator for 1 hour to chill.

Heat half the oil in a large frying pan over medium-high heat. Fry the meatballs in batches for 12 minutes each, turning frequently to ensure they're thoroughly cooked through. Add more oil as needed.

Serve them hot garnished with parsley and lemon wedges on the side.

50 MIN

Chicken and Black Olive Tagine

1 tbsp ras el hanout (see recipe page 272)

700g (1½ lb) chicken breasts, cut into 2cm (1in) chunks

1 x 400g (14oz) can diced tomatoes

1 cup (140g, 5oz) black olives, pitted and halved

4 tbsps preserved lemon, diced

½ cup (60g, 2oz) almonds, roughly chopped

STAPLES

3 tbsps olive oil

1¼ cups (300ml, 10fl oz) water (or use chicken stock)

Freshly ground salt and pepper

OPTIONAL

3 cloves garlic, crushed

⅔ cup (125g, 4oz) dried apricots, chopped

Fresh parsley, chopped, to garnish

Heat the oil in a large heatproof tagine (or heatproof casserole dish) over medium heat. Fry the garlic, if using, and ras el hanout for 2 minutes. Increase the heat to medium-high and add fry the chicken in batches for 5 minutes until browned then return all the chicken to the tagine.

Stir through the tomatoes, olives, apricots, if using, and preserved lemon, then pour in the water (or stock) and bring to a boil. Reduce heat to low and simmer, covered, for 30 minutes. Stir through the almonds and simmer for another 5 minutes uncovered.

Season to taste and serve garnished with parsley.

40 MIN

Moroccan Potato Salad with Olives

800g (1¾ lb) potatoes, peeled and cut into 2cm (1in) chunks (use Bintje or Desiree)

2 cups (280g, 10oz) Kalamata olives, pitted

¼ cup (35g, 1¼ oz) capers, drained, liquid reserved

2 lemons; 1 juiced, 1 cut into wedges

STAPLES

⅓ cup (80ml, 3fl oz) extra virgin olive oil

1 tbsp apple cider vinegar

Freshly ground salt and pepper

Boil the potatoes in lightly salted water for about 10 minutes until tender.

Drain and rinse with cold water and place in a large salad bowl. Let cool for 25 minutes.

Add the olives and capers.

Whisk together 1 tablespoon lemon juice, the olive oil, vinegar and a couple of grinds of salt and pepper. Drizzle over the salad and toss to combine.

Add more lemon juice and salt and pepper to taste.

Serve with lemon wedges on the side.

1 HR, 15 MIN

Chicken Tagine

4 cloves garlic, crushed

1½ tbsps Moroccan spice mix

800g (1¾ lb) chicken breasts cut into 2cm (1in) cubes

4 cups (540g, 1¼ lb) pumpkin, cut into 2cm (1in) chunks

¾ cup (120g, 4oz) dried cranberries

3 cups (750ml, 24fl oz) chicken stock

STAPLES

3 tbsps olive oil

Freshly ground salt and pepper

OPTIONAL

Fresh mint leaves, torn, for garnish

Heat the oil in a large heatproof tagine (or heatproof casserole dish) over medium heat. Fry the garlic and spice mix for 2 minutes. Increase the heat to medium-high and fry the chicken in batches for 5 minutes until browned then return all the chicken to the tagine.

Stir through the pumpkin and cranberries, then pour the stock and bring to a boil. Reduce heat to low and simmer, covered, for 30 minutes.

Remove the lid, season and simmer for another 15 minutes or until the pumpkin is soft.

Season further to taste and serve hot, garnished with mint leaves, if desired.

Moroccan Tomato and Lentil Soup

4 cloves garlic, crushed

2 tbsps ras el hanout (shop-bought or see recipe page 272)

3 cups (400g, 14oz) pumpkin, cut into 1½ cm (¾ in) chunks

2 x 400g (14oz) cans diced tomatoes

1 cup (185g, 6oz) red lentils, rinsed

3 cups (400g, 14oz) tightly packed kale, stems trimmed, chopped

STAPLES

2 tbsps olive oil

4½ cups (1.25L, 38fl oz) water (or use vegetable stock)

Freshly ground salt and pepper

Heat the oil in a large pot over medium heat. Fry the garlic and ras el hanout for 2 minutes.

Add the pumpkin and cook for 2 minutes. Pour in the tomatoes, lentils and water (or stock) and bring to a boil.

Reduce to a simmer and cook, covered, for 15 minutes. Stir the kale through and simmer for a further 10 minutes or until the lentils are tender.

Scoop out 1 cup of the mixture and use a stick blender to puree it until smooth. Return the puree to the pot and stir through.

Season the soup to taste and serve hot.

20 MIN

Spicy Moroccan Prawns

700g (1½ lb) prawn tails, peeled and deveined

2 tbsps fresh ginger, minced

5 cloves garlic, crushed

3 tbsps ras el hanout (shop-bought or see recipe page 272)

½ tbsp ground cumin

1 tbsp lemon juice

STAPLES

⅓ cup (80ml, 3fl oz) extra virgin olive oil

Freshly ground salt and pepper

OPTIONAL

Fresh parsley, chopped, to garnish

Heat the oil in a large frying pan over medium heat. Fry the ginger for 30 seconds then add the garlic and fry for 1 minute.

Add the ras el hanout, cumin and a couple of grinds of salt and pepper and fry for another 1 minute. Increase the heat to medium-high and fry the prawns in batches for around 4 minutes, turning halfway, until cooked through.

Serve the prawns with lemon juice drizzled over the top and garnished with parsley.

15 MIN

1.5 CUPS

Chermoula

1 cup (45g, 1½ oz) flat-leaf parsley leaves, roughly chopped

6 large cloves garlic, crushed

1 tsp ground cumin

1 green chilli, seeded and roughly chopped

⅓ cup (100ml, 3½ fl oz) lemon juice

STAPLES

½ cup (110ml, 4fl oz) olive oil

1½ tsps salt

Freshly ground pepper

Place all the ingredients in a blender or use a stick blender to combine everything into a thick sauce.

Season to taste with salt and pepper.

45 MIN

Roast Beetroot and Chickpea Za'atar Yoghurt

8 medium beetroots, peeled and quartered

2 x 400g (14oz) cans chickpeas, drained and rinsed

¼ cup (10g, ¼ oz) za'atar mix (shop-bought or see recipe page 148), reserve 1 tbsp

2 cups (500ml, 1pt) Greek yoghurt

½ cup (125ml, 4fl oz) tahini sauce (shop-bought or see recipe page 118)

½ cup (20g, ¾ oz) mint leaves, torn

STAPLES

3 tbsps olive oil

Freshly ground salt and pepper

OPTIONAL

1 tbsp ground cumin, to garnish

Preheat the oven to 200°C (400°F, Gas Mark 6) and line a large baking tray with baking paper.

Place the beetroot and chickpeas in a large bowl and toss together with the za'atar, olive oil and a couple of grinds of salt and pepper.

Place the beetroot only on the baking tray and roast for 15 minutes. Remove the tray from the oven, turn the beetroot pieces over and scatter the chickpeas around them. Roast for 15 more minutes or until the beetroot is tender.

Whisk together the yoghurt and tahini sauce.

To serve, place equal portions of the yoghurt in serving bowls, top with beetroot and chickpeas and sprinkle over the reserved za'atar, cumin (if desired) and mint leaves.

20 MIN

Harissa Salmon on Couscous

2 cups (380g, 14oz) couscous

3 cups (750ml, 24fl oz) vegetable stock

4 x 200g (7oz) salmon fillets, skin on

¼ cup (65g, 2oz) harissa paste (shop-bought or see recipe page 264)

STAPLES

1 tbsp butter

2 tbsps olive oil

Freshly ground salt and pepper

OPTIONAL

Fresh parsley, roughly chopped, to garnish

1 lemon, cut into wedges

Place the couscous and butter in a large pot and pour the stock over and bring to a boil. Turn the heat off and let the couscous sit, covered, to absorb the liquid.

Rub the oil and harissa paste into the salmon fillets along with a grind or two of salt and pepper.

Heat a non-stick frying pan over medium heat and fry the salmon fillets, skin side down, for 3 minutes. Then turn over and cook for another 2 minutes or until cooked to preferred doneness.

Fluff up the couscous with a fork and season to taste.

Serve the salmon on a bed of couscous with parsley sprinkled over the top and lemon wedges on the side.

**20 MIN
+ COOLING**

Crunchy
Couscous Salad

2 cups (380g, 14oz)
couscous

3 cups (750ml, 24fl
oz) vegetable stock

1 large red
capsicum, seeded
and chopped

1 large yellow
capsicum, seeded
and chopped

1 tbsp lemon juice

⅔ cup (30g, 1oz)
parsley, finely
chopped

STAPLES

1 tbsp butter

2 tbsps olive oil

Freshly ground salt
and pepper

Place the couscous and butter in a large pot
and pour the stock over and bring to a boil.
Turn the heat off and let the couscous sit for
10 minutes, covered, to absorb the liquid.

Whisk together the lemon juice, olive oil
and a couple of grinds of salt and pepper.
Pour over the chopped capsicums and
toss to coat.

Fluff up the couscous with a fork and season
to taste. Let it cool for at least 30 minutes.

Place the couscous, then the capsicums and
parsley in a large bowl. Stir to mix through
and serve.

50 MIN + CHILLING

Moroccan-Style Fish Balls

800g (1¾ lb) flathead fillets, boned, skin removed

3 potatoes, peeled and cubed

1 onion, grated and squeezed to remove excess liquid

2 cups (250g, 8oz) breadcrumbs

4 tbsps parsley, finely chopped

1 tbsp ras el hanout (shop-bought or see recipe page 272)

STAPLES

3 large eggs, lightly beaten

1 tbsp milk

Freshly ground salt and pepper

Vegetable oil, for frying

Steam the fish for 8 minutes until cooked. Boil the potatoes for 10 minutes in lightly salted water until tender, then drain and rinse in cold water.

Flake the fish into a large bowl and mash together with the potato, onion, 1 tablespoon breadcrumbs, parsley, half the ras el hanout, ½ tablespoon beaten egg, milk and salt and pepper. Form into 2½ cm (1in) wide balls and place in the fridge for 1 hour.

Mix the remaining breadcrumbs and ras el hanout and spread out in a shallow dish. Place the egg in a separate shallow dish. Dredge the balls in the egg then the breadcrumbs.

Heat 2cm (1in) of oil in a deep-sided frying pan and fry the balls for 6 minutes until browned. Drain on paper towels.

45 MIN

Grilled Eggplant

4 large eggplants cut into 1cm (½ in) thick slices

1 x 400g (14oz) can diced tomatoes, drained

¾ cup (185g, 6oz) chermoula (shop-bought or see recipe page 297)

2 tbsps ras el hanout (shop-bought or see recipe page 272)

½ tsp sweet paprika

STAPLES

⅓ cup (100ml, 3½ fl oz) olive oil

Freshly ground salt and pepper

OPTIONAL

Fresh parsley, chopped, to garnish

Preheat the oven to 200°C (400°F, Gas Mark 6). Line two large baking trays with baking paper.

Brush the slices with olive oil. Arrange them on the baking trays and bake for 20 minutes until cooked through.

Heat 1 tablespoon olive oil in a small frying pan over medium heat. Add the tomatoes, chermoula, ras el hanout and paprika and cook for 10 minutes.

Place half of the cooked eggplants in a bowl and mash to a pulp. Add to the spiced tomatoes and stir through. Season to taste.

Combine the eggplants and sauce together in a large bowl.

Serve hot or cold, garnished with parsley if desired.

1 HR

Fregola Sarda with Caramelised Pumpkin

1 large butternut pumpkin, cut into 2cm (1in) wide slices

¼ cup (60g, 2oz) chermoula (shop-bought or see recipe page 297)

200g (7oz) fregola (or use pearl couscous)

½ cup (15g, ½ oz) baby spinach leaves, finely chopped

1 large lemon, juiced

sprigs parsley leaves, to garnish

STAPLES

¼ cup (60ml, 2fl oz) plus 2 tbsps olive oil

Freshly ground salt and pepper

OPTIONAL

Fresh parsley sprigs, to garnish

Preheat the oven to 180°C (350°F, Gas Mark 4) and line two large baking trays with baking paper.

Place the pumpkin slices in a large bowl and toss to coat with ¼ cup olive oil and 2 teaspoons each of salt and pepper. Arrange on the baking trays and bake for 20 minutes, then remove from the oven and flip the pieces over. Return to the oven to bake for a further 20 minutes until slightly browned and caramelised on top.

Bring a large pot of lightly salted water to the boil. Add the fregola and boil for 15 minutes or until cooked through.

Drain and put into a bowl with the spinach, 1 tablespoon lemon juice and 2 tablespoons olive oil.

To serve, arrange pieces of pumpkin over a bed of fregola, drizzle the chermoula over the top and garnish with parsley leaves.

3HR, 15 MIN

Beef and Preserved Lemon Tagine

1kg (2lb) beef cheek, trimmed, cut into 4cm (1½ in) chunks

4 large cloves garlic, crushed

1½ tbsps ground cumin

1½ tbsps ground coriander

2 tsps dried chilli flakes

⅓ cup (85g, 3oz) preserved lemon, chopped

STAPLES

⅓ cup (100ml, 3½ fl oz) olive oil

2 tsps salt

2 tsps ground pepper

¼ cup (60ml, 2fl oz) water

OPTIONAL

Cooked couscous, to serve

Fresh coriander leaves, to garnish

Mix together ¼ cup olive oil, garlic, cumin, coriander, chilli, salt and pepper into a thick paste. Place the beef in a bowl, add the paste and toss to coat.

Heat the remaining oil in a large heatproof tagine (or heatproof casserole dish) over medium heat. Fry the beef in batches for 5 minutes until browned. Add the water, turn the heat down to low and cook, covered, for 3 hours, until nearly falling apart, adding more water as needed to prevent it from doing dry.

Remove the beef from the tagine and use two forks to shred it. Mix the lemon through the beef and season further to taste.

Serve on a bed of couscous, garnished with coriander leaves.

Moroccan Beef Meatball Skewers

700g (1½ lb) minced beef

1 onion, grated and squeezed to remove excess liquid

2 tbsps fresh mint, finely chopped

2 tsps ground cumin

2 tsps sweet paprika

1 cup (250g, 9oz) cacik (see recipe page 185 or use Greek yoghurt)

12 wooden skewers, soaked in hot water for 30 minutes

STAPLES

1 egg, lightly beaten

Freshly ground salt and pepper

3 tbsps olive oil

Place the beef, grated onion, mint, cumin, paprika, egg and a couple of good grinds of salt and pepper in a large bowl and thoroughly mix together.

Mould small amounts of the mixture into balls roughly 2½ cm (1in) in diameter.

Thread the meatballs onto the skewers and brush with olive oil.

Heat a grill pan over medium-high heat and grill the meatballs in batches for 10 minutes, turning frequently until cooked through.

Serve hot, with cacik (or yoghurt) on the side.

20 MIN
+ COOLING

Traditional Carrot Salad

500g (1lb) carrots, peeled, halved lengthways and sliced

4 large cloves garlic, finely chopped

3 tbsps chermoula (shop-bought or see recipe page 297)

1 tsp ground cumin

STAPLES

3 tbsps olive oil

2 tbsps apple cider vinegar

Freshly ground salt and pepper

Place the carrots in large saucepan, cover with water, add 1 teaspoon salt and bring to a boil. Reduce heat to low and simmer for 10 minutes until tender. Drain and let cool for 1 hour.

Heat the oil in a small frying pan over medium heat and fry the garlic for 1 minute. Add the chermoula, cumin and vinegar and fry for 2 more minutes then remove from heat and let cool for 20 minutes.

Place the carrots in a large salad bowl, drizzle the chermoula mix over the top and toss to coat the carrots. Season to taste and serve.

40 MIN

Carrots with Fruity Cauliflower Couscous

1 large head
cauliflower

1 bunch baby
carrots, tops
trimmed

1 cup (160g, 6oz)
sultanas

⅔ cup (80g, 3oz)
almonds, roughly
chopped

¼ cup (40g, 1½ oz)
sesame seeds

1 tbsp ground
cumin

STAPLES

⅓ cup (80ml, 3fl oz)
olive oil

1 tbsp red wine vinegar

Freshly ground salt
and pepper

OPTIONAL

Fresh mint leaves,
to garnish

½ cup (125ml, 4fl oz)
Greek yoghurt,
to garnish

Preheat oven to 180°C (350°F, Gas Mark
4) and line a large baking tray with baking
paper.

Toss the carrots with half the olive oil
and a couple of grinds of salt and pepper.
Arrange in one layer on the tray and bake
for 20 minutes until tender.

Break the cauliflower into florets and steam
for 10 minutes. Place in a food processor
and pulse until they're broken down to the
size of couscous grains. Place in a large
bowl and toss with the sultanas, almonds,
half the sesame seeds, the remaining oil
and the vinegar. Season to taste.

Serve the carrots on top of the couscous
with the remaining sesame seeds and cumin
sprinkled over the top. Garnish with mint
leaves and yoghurt on the side.

50 MIN

Moroccan Spiced Chicken with Eggplant and Dates

1kg (2lb) chicken thighs, skin on, bone in

1 large onion, chopped

12 Medjool dates, pitted and chopped

2 large eggplants, cut into 1½ cm (¾ in) cubes

2 tbsps harissa (shop-bought or see recipe page 264)

2 cups (500ml, 1pt) chicken stock

STAPLES

¼ cup (60ml, 2fl oz) olive oil

Freshly ground salt and pepper

OPTIONAL

Cooked rice, to serve

2 tsps paprika, to garnish

¼ cup (30g, 1oz) pistachios, chopped, to garnish

Preheat the oven to 200°C (400°F, Gas Mark 6).

Rub the chicken skins with ½ tablespoon of salt.

Heat half the oil in a large heatproof casserole dish and fry the onion for 5 minutes.

Add the dates and eggplant and fry for 5 more minutes.

Remove from the heat and stir through the harissa and stock. Sit the chicken pieces snugly on top, skin side up, and drizzle with the remaining olive oil.

Bake uncovered for 35 minutes or until the chicken is crisped on top and cooked through. Season the dates and eggplants to taste.

To serve, arrange the eggplant mixture on a bed of cooked rice and sit the chicken pieces on top, sprinkled with paprika and chopped pistachios, if desired.

1 HR, 20 MIN

Orange Blossom Cake

200g (7oz) almond meal

1 large orange, zested and juiced

2 tbsps orange blossom water

¼ cup (30g, 1oz) flaked almonds, chopped

4 medium eggs, room temperature

STAPLES

230g (8oz) unsalted butter, room temperature

1 cup (230g, 8oz) caster sugar

½ cup (60g, 2oz) plain flour

½ tsp vanilla essence

Preheat oven to 180°C (350°F, Gas Mark 4) and line a 22cm (8½ in) springform tin with lightly greased baking paper.

Beat the butter and sugar together until it looks like whipped cream. Add the eggs one at a time, ensuring each is thoroughly mixed in before adding the next. Add the flour, then mix through the almond meal, zest, juice, orange blossom water and vanilla.

Pour the mixture into the cake tin and bake for 1 hour in the lower third of the oven. The cake is cooked when a skewer inserted into the middle comes out clean.

Let the cake rest for 5 minutes before removing from the tin to a cake rack to cool for 1 hour.

Garnish with flaked almonds to serve.

COOKIES

Moroccan Shortbread Cookies

2 tsps sesame oil

1½ tsps orange blossom water

¼ cup (30g, 1oz) almond meal

1 cup (175g, 6oz) fine semolina

STAPLES

1⅓ cup (280g, 10oz) caster sugar

100g (3½ oz) unsalted butter, room temperature

3 medium eggs, room temperature

½ tsp vanilla extract

1½ cups (185g, 6oz) self-raising flour

Preheat the oven to 175°C (350°F, Gas Mark 4) and line two large baking trays with baking paper.

Beat together the sugar and butter until it resembles whipped cream. Add the eggs one at a time, ensuring each is thoroughly mixed in before adding the next. Then mix through the sesame oil, orange blossom water and vanilla. Next, mix through the almond meal, semolina and self-raising flour in turn until thoroughly combined.

Form tablespoons of dough into balls then place about 5cm (2in) apart on the trays and flatten slightly.

Bake for 15 minutes or until golden. Let them cool for 5 minutes, then remove them to a wire rack to cool.

25 MIN
+ FREEZING

Strawberry and Rose Water Icy Poles

2 cups (400g, 14oz) strawberries, hulled and roughly chopped

1 x 400ml (14fl oz) can coconut milk

2 tsps rose water

1½ cups (375ml, 13fl oz) thickened cream

100g (3½ oz) white cooking chocolate

12 icy-pole moulds

12 icy-pole sticks

STAPLES

3 tbsps caster sugar

Place three-quarters of the strawberries in a blender with the coconut milk, rose water, sugar and 1 cup of the cream and blend until smooth.

Mix the rest of the strawberries through and pour equal amounts into the icy pole moulds and place in the freezer for 1 hour.

Remove and stick the icy pole sticks in about halfway up the sticks.

Freeze for at least another 5 hours until solid.

In a small saucepan over low heat stir together the remaining cream and white chocolate until smooth. Do not increase the heat or the chocolate will burn.

Drizzle the melted chocolate over the icy poles, let it harden and serve.

index

First Published in 2018 by Herron Book Distributors Pty Ltd
14 Manton St
Morningside
QLD 4170
www.herronbooks.com

Custom book production by Captain Honey Pty Ltd
12 Station St
Bangalow
NSW 2479
www.captainhoney.com.au

Cataloguing-in-Publication. A catalogue record for this book is
available from the National Library of Australia

ISBN 978-0-947163-69-3

Front cover image by Tatyana Malova © Shutterstock.com
Page 10 photo by Brigette Lucas
All other images used under license from Shutterstock.com
Printed and bound in China by 1010 Printing International Limited

5 4 3 2   19 20 21 22

NOTES FOR THE READER

All reasonable efforts have been made to ensure the accuracy of the
content in this book. Information in this book is not intended as a
substitute for medical advice. The author and publisher cannot and
do not accept any legal duty of care or responsibility in relation to the
content in this book, and disclaim any liabilities relating to its use.